Rudyard Kipling

Twayne's English Authors Series

Kinley E. Roby, Editor
Northeastern University

TEAS 339

RUDYARD KIPLING
(1865-1936)
Courtesy of the
National Portrait
Gallery, London.

Rudyard Kipling

By James Harrison

University of Guelph
College of Arts

Twayne Publishers • *Boston*

Library of Congress Cataloging in Publication Data

Harrison, James, 1927-
  Rudyard Kipling.

  (Twayne's English authors series : TEAS 339)
  Bibliography: p. 163
  Includes index.
  1. Kipling, Rudyard, 1865-1936
—Criticism and interpretation.
I. Title. II. Series.
PR 4857.H28   828'.91209   82-1999
ISBN 0-8057-6825-4   AACR2

To my mother
and the memory of my father

Contents

About the Author

James Harrison is a professor at the University of Guelph, Guelph, Ontario. Born in Sri Lanka, he was educated in India and England, where he taught for a number of years before coming to Canada. He has brought out a book of poems, edited an anthology of scientific writing, and published articles on a variety of subjects, mainly in the field of Victorian literature.

Preface

If anyone had told me, in my immoderate youth, that time would one day see me writing a book on Kipling, I should have laughed in his face. For, after a childhood spent in Ceylon and India, I was to become, once the family had returned to Britain, as rabid in my antiimperialism as Kipling had ever been in his imperialism. Kipling's views had by that time, of course, fallen into disfavor. So, fashionable in my unbelief as he had earlier been in his belief, I dismissed him with all the lofty scorn of enlightened adolescence. By a nice touch of irony I was unaware of at the time, this all began while I was still a student at the school his father and maternal grandfather had attended. Either the school authorities did not know of this claim to fame, or they preferred not to noise it abroad.

Naturally I based my judgment on a minimum of firsthand knowledge, as was probably true, and may well still be true, of most of his severest detractors. It was not until many years later that I began discovering the bulk of what he had written. And I was still strongly repelled by many of the social and political attitudes to be found therein. By that time, however, most of the British Empire had all but disappeared. So discredited were the old imperialistic axioms, moreover, that most of the nation states it broke up into did not even have to fight for their independence. So it is possible, by now, to regard the opinions Kipling expresses with a kind of historical detachment. They seem almost as remote as Shakespeare's views on kingship, Milton's on the status of women, or Defoe's on an earlier stage of imperialism.

It is possible from such a detached position, moreover, to see that Kipling's attitudes were a good deal more complex and equivocal than one would ever guess from much of what has been said about him. He clearly knew and loved the India of the Indians, for instance, as few of the Englishmen he mixed with did. And his own attitudes were often much more liberal than those he attibuted to his characters. In addition, once the ideological obstacles have been circumvented, it becomes apparent what a remarkably gifted writer Kipling was, with how extraordinary a range of theme, technique, and tone.

We might have guessed as much, of course, from the enormous popularity he achieved during his lifetime. Even in America publishers stumbled over one another to bring out both official and pirated editions, and in Britain most of his books have never been out of print. Yet the very fact that he has been able to appeal to so wide a readership, in many instances doubtless on other than the purest aesthetic grounds, has sometimes been held against him. And it must be admitted that Kipling is now and then guilty of a certain distasteful antiintellectualism, seeming to denigrate mind and spirit as against the world of action. He has even been felt to deprecate his own gifts as an artist, as compared with the skills and mysteries of such practical callings as engineer or surgeon. This is not fair comment, however, except insofar as Kipling always emphasizes the artist's role as craftsman, as maker, rather than as prophet or seer.

Indeed, one of my major problems, in writing this study of a journalist turned journeyman of letters, with an output of three novels, between two and three hundred short stories, and well over five hundred poems, has been how to do justice to such a diverse volume of work. I have assumed that many of those likely to read this book will not be familiar with more than a handful of stories, about the same number of poems, and maybe *Captains Courageous* or *Kim*. Accordingly I have summarized content where this seemed necessary for an understanding of comment or analysis, which has clearly raised problems because of the sheer number of separate works considered. In the case of the fiction, on which I place my main emphasis, I have divided Kipling's career into an early or Indian, a middle, and a late period, so as to show both continuity and development. Within each period, however, I have grouped stories thematically, so as to emphasize recurring preoccupations.

I have used Scribner's *Outward Bound Edition* for the fiction, as the most convenient uniform American edition available to me. Its one major disadvantage is that some stories appear in volumes they are not accustomed to finding themselves in . I have accordingly indicated, in the index, the title of the volume in which each story referred to appears, first in the *Outward Bound*, and second (if different) in the Macmillan and Doubleday editions.

I should like to thank those of my colleagues who have offered much needed advice and encouragement, the University of Guelph library staff for their patient and invaluable cooperation, and my editor for both his decisiveness and his tact. I also acknowledge, gratefully, the permission of the National Trust of Great Britain, Macmillan of London Ltd., and Doubleday and Company Inc., New York, to quote from the works of Kipling.

James Harrison

University of Guelph

Chronology

1898	*The Day's Work.*
1899	*Stalky & Co.* Last visit to USA. Death of Josephine, his eldest child.
1900-1908	January to March in South Africa every year.
1901	*Kim.*
1902	*Just So Stories.* Moved to "Bateman's," Sussex.
1903	*The Five Nations* (poems).
1904	*Traffics and Discoveries.*
1906	*Puck of Pook's Hill.*
1907	Nobel Prize for Literature.
1909	*Actions and Reactions.*
1910	*Rewards and Fairies.*
1913	Voyage to Egypt. *Letters of Travel. Songs from Books.*
1915	John Kipling, his son, missing, believed killed, in France.
1917	*A Diversity of Creatures.*
1919	*The Years Between* (poems).
1923	*Land and Sea Tales for Scouts and Guides. The Irish Guards in the Great War.*
1926	*Debits and Credits.*
1927	Voyage to Brazil. *Brazilian Sketches.*
1930	*Thy Servant a Dog.* Voyage to West Indies.
1932	*Limits and Renewals.*
1936	Death of Rudyard Kipling.
1937	*Something of Myself* published posthumously.

Chapter One
Biography

Rudyard Kipling began his adult life as a journalist, and most of his remaining years were spent, rather as a journalist's are, scribbling in the margins of a life of action. It was men of action he most admired, mixed most easily with, most valued the good opinion of, and wrote most often about. As at least one biographer has pointed out,[1] whereas Thomas Hardy's pallbearers were all poets or dramatists, Kipling, the next to be buried in Westminster Abbey's Poet's Corner, had a prime minister, an admiral, a general, and the master of a Cambridge college to help carry him there. Much more seems to have happened in Kipling's life, therefore, than in those of most writers. The mere list of countries he lived in (India, England, the United States, South Africa) or visited (Canada, Australia, New Zealand, Japan, France, Belgium, Spain, Algeria, Brazil, Jamaica, Czechoslovakia, Palestine, Mesopotamia) confirms this impression. Yet it is clear, if one takes a closer look, that what he actually did during most of this busy life was to write.

Kipling was born of good, middle-class Methodist stock, from Yorkshire on his father, John Lockwood Kipling's, side, and on his mother, Alice Macdonald's, from Scotland, Ireland, and Wales. John Kipling was for a time a designer and modeler for a Staffordshire pottery firm, and then an assistant to an architectural sculptor in London, where he worked on the new Museum of Art (now the Victoria and Albert Museum). In marrying Alice he became part of a peculiarly close-knit family which, though not of noticeably superior social origins to the Kiplings, was in the process of doing well for itself. Two of Alice's sisters were already married to artists (Agnes to Edward Poynter, later President of the Royal Academy, and Georgina to the well-known Pre-Raphaelite Burne-Jones). The third, Louisa, was to marry a wealthy industrialist, Alfred Baldwin, and become mother of a future prime minister. In such company, a struggling apprentice craftsman must have seemed, or must have felt himself to be, a poor catch. Bride and groom were, in fact, twenty-eight before they felt able to marry. What finally made this possible was the offer of work at Jeejeebyhoy School of Art in Bombay. And it has widely been assumed that his future brother-in-law, Burne-Jones, helped John Kipling (or Lockwood Kipling as he was hereafter known) to obtain the post. Be that as it may, one of the attractions of the position must have been to escape just such an atmosphere of patronage. So it was in Bombay, in December 1865, that Rudyard was born.

By all accounts he led an idyllically happy early childhood. He was a veritable young rajah among the household servants, as well as having unusually indulgent parents for those days. But most of his time was spent with his ayah (a Roman Catholic) and the other servants, visiting church or temple indifferently, speaking "the vernacular" more fluently than English, even having to be reminded by the servants to speak English when he went in to see his parents.[2] T. S. Eliot sees this first period of early childhood in India as the time when Kipling came to love the country, and the second, of early manhood, as that when he acquired his imperialist paternalism.[3] In a sense this is undoubtedly true. Yet, in another, a child of four or five whose merest whim is law to the adult servants around him is already a fully fledged Anglo-Indian.[4] (The term is used in this book, as it was in India at that time, for an Englishman living and working in India. Those of mixed race were known as Eurasians.)

Sooner or later even the broad-minded Kiplings must have felt that their half-heathen offspring needed a more British background. In addition, the Indian climate presented a perpetual health hazard to European (and doubtless also Indian) children. So in 1871 the Kiplings took the step that nearly all Anglo-Indian families had to take, sooner or later. They brought their children home to England for six months, and left them there when they returned to India. Rudyard was rising six, his sister just over three.

For middle-class children above a certain age to spend much of the year in boarding school has long been more the accepted thing in Britain than America. And most Anglo-Indian children were sent home to aunts or grandparents some years before starting at such a school. What seems harder to forgive is that the Kiplings left their children, not with one or other of Alice's sisters, but with strangers who advertised their services in a newspaper. There is some evidence, however, that Rudyard, whose behavior was far more headstrong and vocal than was acceptable in Victorian children, would not have been entirely welcome at any of his aunts' or uncles' houses. So a major factor influencing the decision may well have been the pride of poor relations unwilling to beg for favors.

Certainly the Kiplings had no knowledge that their children were particularly unhappy. Alice's family visited them in Southsea, the seaside town where they were boarded, a few months after their parents had set sail, and formed a very favorable impression of Captain and Mrs. Holloway, the couple looking after them. Yet that Rudyard in particular suffered deeply there can be no doubt. For this we have his own direct word on the matter in his otherwise singularly reticent autobiography, *Something of Myself*. Almost more conclusive, there is the repeated testimony of two uniquely autobiographical episodes in his fiction—the short story "Baa Baa Black Sheep" and the opening chapter in his novel *The Light that Failed*. Finally, there are his sister's memories in old age.[5] At first Captain Holloway, who took quite a liking to the boy and would go for walks with him and tell him stories of life at sea, was some protection. But after the captain's death, nothing stood between Rudyard and Mrs. Holloway's deep dislike of him as a spoiled, ill-mannered, precocious, headstrong, clumsy boy who was used to having servants at his beck and call. Trix, his sister, she took to her heart, having never had and perhaps always wanted a daughter. But she and her son, some six years Rudyard's senior, combined forces to make the boy's life a misery. He would be interrogated as to his day's doings and then punished for any misdemeanor, not only physically but with threats of the much more terrible penalties in store for him in a Calvinistic Hell. Later, when Rudyard's already weak eyesight deteriorated seriously and his schoolwork suffered, he was punished for this also. And when he destroyed one of the monthly bad reports from school and denied he had ever received it, he was made to wear a placard round his neck bearing the word "LIAR."[6]

There were, of course, breaks in such a leaden sky—holidays spent with the Burne-Joneses, in a house filled with paintings and statues and wallpaper and people such as would have confirmed all the pious Mrs. Holloway's deepest convictions that Rudyard was a lost soul. For the Christmas of 1873, for instance, the Burne-Jones children and Rudyard were joined by the two daughters of William Morris (Uncle Topsy to the children). They were then entertained with stories, songs, games, comic drawings, even a magic lantern show, and general high jinks devised and executed by some of the brightest spirits of late Victorian England. As soon as they were old enough, moreover, the children were encouraged to create their own pictures, stories, plays. In later years Rudyard and his cousins, together with May Morris, would produce their own magazine.

Such interludes were always darkened for Rudyard, of course, by the approaching return to the House of Desolation, as he later referred to his Southsea prison. Yet never did either child divulge the true state of affairs there. Only when Rudyard started running into trees he had not noticed did Georgina grow alarmed, consult an eye specialist, and send for his mother. On her arrival from India, without warning, she went in to kiss Rudyard good night, and he threw up his arm to ward off the expected blow.[7]

Clearly this period of Kipling's life, months of barren gloom alternating with brief weeks of intense, rich joy, must have left its mark on his emerging personality. The pattern of alternating happiness and unhappiness was not yet broken, moreover. After what R. G. Collingwood describes as "the happiest year of young Rudyard's life,"[8] he was again left in England, this time at a boarding school, while his mother rejoined her husband. At the end of the first term, which Kipling freely admits "was horrible," he had to remain at school for the holidays.

I expected the worst, but when we survivors were left in the echoing form-rooms after the others had driven cheering to the station, life suddenly became a new thing.... The big remote seniors turned into tolerant elder brothers, and let us small fry rove far out of bounds; shared their delicacies with us at tea; and even took an interest in our hobbies. We had no special work to do and enjoyed ourselves hugely. On the return of the school "all smiles stopped together," which was right and proper. (36:24–25)

The rightness and properness of having to pay for one's pleasures in this way, of subjecting them to a controlling discipline, is characteristic of Kipling's whole philosophy of life. Yet so is the rightness and properness of enjoying oneself, of kicking over the traces, of challenging the law before resubmitting to its yoke. To talk of the Apollonian and Dionysian aspects of a work like *Stalky & Co.*, the Olympian detachment of the cane-wielding headmaster counterbalancing the anarchic energy of those he must beat, would clearly. be ridiculous. Yet just such fruitful tensions between youth and age, ritual and spontaneity, anarchy and law, the letter and the spirit are at work in much of Kipling's best writing. And that they are is in part a direct legacy from Kipling's childhood, and in part a tribute to his ability to survive that childhood. She never broke his spirit, that keeper of the House of Desolation. The loyalty of his sister, a month's bliss every Christmas, and above all the books he learned to escape into, helped him find the necessary resources within himself to endure the worst she could do. Nor, on the other hand, did she cripple him equally for life by turning him into a permanent and petulant rebel.

Children from authoritarian homes all too often grow up to be authoritarian conformist adults. The relationships this leads to are the only ones they have learned to be a part of. And this, as will emerge, is to a large extent true of Kipling in his public and political attitudes. Yet his parents proper were, if anything, indulgent. And so was Kipling as a parent, leaving the management and control of things largely to his wife. Only in his life as an artist did he strike a balance between these two extremes, repeatedly setting the one off against the other in the themes he chose to handle.

Kipling's own assessment of what happened was that those dark years "drained me of any capacity for real, personal hate for the rest of my days" (36:17). One might well question whether any known psychological mechanism would have this effect; certainly his fiction is that of a man who knows how to hate and, as a redeeming corollary, to forgive. What seems more likely is that he learned all too well the self-protective trick of suppressing the angry response. In addition, the bitter sense of having been betrayed, which both children clearly felt during the first few months, probably left them too insecure emotionally to feel at ease about trusting themselves to indulge in strong feelings of any kind. So the harmonious relationship he seems to have been able to renew quite readily with both his parents, after each long period of separation, was in all likelihood a gift horse he did not care to look too closely in the mouth. Instead, the private fortress of family life, at first with his parents in India and later with his wife and children, and the public fortress of law and order which he demanded of society, became his defenses against an encompassing darkness the sense of which he acquired early and never lost.

The school he attended, the United Services College (USC) in Westward Ho, Devon, was a new one. It had been founded for the express purpose of getting the sons of officers through the recently established examinations for entry to military academies such as Sandhurst and Woolwich. Most of the students were there because their fathers could not afford to send them to more prestigious schools; some were there because they had been expelled from such for academic or other reasons. Therefore the atmosphere was tough and the fees were low—one reason at least why Kipling was sent there. A better reason was that the headmaster or principal belonged to the intellectual circle already known to Rudyard from his visits to the Burne-Joneses. Cormell Price (Uncle Crom) was an unlikely choice for the post in that his social and political views were so much more radical than those of most of his pupils' parents. But he had an excellent reputation as a teacher. And so single-mindedly did the school concentrate on preparing its unpromising material for those all-important examinations that developing the boys' moral and social attitudes in the approved "Rugby" manner was a luxury it could ill afford.

One result was that, after surviving a year or more of fairly severe bullying at what was undoubtedly a rough school, Kipling found it more tolerant of eccentrics than the average public school would have been. As in the fictionalized account Kipling gives us of the school in *Stalky & Co.*, a trio of nonconformists shared a study and, three-musketeer-like, stood by one another against all oppression, whether from boys or teachers. The study itself, moreover, with its olive-green and blue stenciled walls, its Greek friezes, and its old glassware, china, and Japanese fans, was a sort of oasis of aestheticism in a redneck wilderness. Not that I wish to imply in any way that Kipling rejected all or most of the assumptions and prejudices of his fellow students. In a debate held just months before he left school, he proposed, overwhelmingly victoriously, "That in the opinion of this Society, the advance of the Russians in Central Asia is hostile to the British Power."[9] But the tolerance of the school as a whole toward unorthodoxy is indicated by the fact that his opponent was no less than the headmaster.

Another result of the school's unusual character was that the curriculum, in many ways much broader than that at most public schools, was geared to getting its students into the army or navy, not Oxford or Cambridge. In any case, though Kipling was always a voracious reader, he never showed signs of conventional academic excellence equal to winning the scholarship he would have needed. So the problem loomed early as to what to do with this shortsighted scribbling laureate of a school for would-be officers. The solution arrived at was to arrange for him to join the staff of the *Civil and Military Gazette*, an English newspaper published in Lahore. Kipling was very much in two minds about the plan. On the one hand he looked forward to rejoining his parents and beginning his adult life; on the other, he was well aware that Lahore was not the center of the literary world. And by this time the one thing that was quite clear to him was that he wanted to be a writer. So, not yet seventeen, and with very mixed feelings, he set sail in September 1882 for the India he had last seen when he was five.

India

The British presence in India had begun, as so often, as a purely commercial venture. What the Hudson Bay Company was to Canada, the British East India Company was to India. With the collapse of the great Mogul Empire in the eighteenth century, however, and the disintegration of the subcontinent into quarreling princedoms, the rival French East India Company began training troops and allying itself with one or other of the warring factions in order to oust the British. The British, under Robert Clive, replied in kind, and continued, even after the French had been routed, to extend the power of the company by similar means. So extensive did its territories become that, in time, the British government had to assume de facto responsibility for administering them, and found itself inexorably involved in extending these, as had the company. No doubt this was at bottom motivated by India's value as a source of raw materials and as a market for Britain's growing industries. But to a surprising extent these early administrators also had a kind of crusading zeal, seeing it as their mission to bring good government and order to a land sadly in need of them. Suttee (the Hindu practice of burning widows on their husbands' funeral pyres) was abolished; the "thugs" (a caste of roving professional murderers) were suppressed; roads, dams, and irrigation projects were constructed; hospitals, schools, and colleges were established; the peace was kept. By today's standards, what was actually accomplished seems pitifully inadequate. (The British were neither the first nor the last to discover that most of what one does in India is pitifully inadequate.) It was also, of course, thoroughly and distastefully paternalistic. But we cannot understand Kipling unless we view the people he writes about as essentially well-meaning, laboring under conditions of real hardship and danger, and often with a sense of heartbreaking powerlessness in the face of flood, famine, disease, or insurmountable religious prejudice.

The India Kipling returned to, then, had Victoria as its empress, and was united and at peace either under her direct rule or under that of a rajah acknowledging her authority. It was also an India in which the spread of education, and of liberal ideals as voiced by such authors as Ruskin, was leading to a new kind of political, as opposed to military, Indian nationalism. Yet at the same time, as more and more Englishmen brought their wives out with them (instead of, as in the easy-going days of the East India Company, taking a native mistress), and as this expatriate white community became more and more closely knit, there was less and less contact between the races. Lahore, however, where the family now lived, was the capital of the Punjab, and the Punjab, as a frontier province annexed a mere thirty years earlier, was in some ways different. Kipling must have heard much talk at the "club" not only of the original conquest and of the heroic days that followed it, when one young army officer might have absolute authority over thousands of square miles, but of continuing skirmishes with border tribesmen, and of the ever-present Russian menace. For, as his editor's only white assistant, in temporary command for several weeks before his seventeenth birthday, he became a man overnight, and as such was entitled to honorary membership of the Punjab Club from the outset.

Clearly, in such circumstances, any seventeen-year-old is going to take his cue from his elders. And in Kipling's case, having been an outsider all his years at Southsea, and only with difficulty established his position and his right to be himself at USC, it must have been doubly important to feel himself accepted. There are numerous reports, however, that in this he was never wholly successful. His very anxiety to be thought well of, to say and do the right thing, to be in the know, did not always help him. And a sharp tongue, together with a turn of wit he sometimes lacked the wit to curb, was an additional handicap to his being admitted unreservedly into this conservative outpost of a conservative society, still living in an earlier and more conservative century.

Moreover, he seems to have haunted the streets and bazaars, both in search of news and out of sheer interest, more than was seemly in a European. He had regained his command of the language quickly, and came near to laying himself open to the charge of actually enjoying the company of Indians.

What we have, then, is a young man still in desperate need of acceptance by his peers, but in an unorthodox profession, with unorthodox tastes and ambitions, and enough intelligence to question some of the very orthodoxies he was so eager to subscribe to and defend. The resulting confusion makes itself apparent, as we shall see, in the fiction he writes about India. His public postures may by and large fit the caricature that has come down to us of an arch imperialist, though such attitudes harden perceptibly after he has left India. But his fiction reveals more ambivalence than he has usually been given credit for.

The pleasures and luxuries of his new life were many. He had his own horse and his own servant—never, on his own admission, dressing, undressing, or shaving himself (this last was done for him while he was still asleep!) until he was twenty-four. But the hardships more than counterbalanced these. There was the ever-present threat of malaria, dysentery, typhoid, and cholera; he faced ten to fifteen hours of drudgery every day, learning his trade from a man who resented having this highfalutin son of a friend of the paper's owner wished on him; and for half the year the heat was all but unbearable, with, for the junior half of the European staff, only the shortest of breaks in the hills. Kipling was subject to insomnia all his days, but never more so than on stifling nights such as he describes in "The City of Dreadful Night," when he would prowl the wakeful city till dawn. And always, whether in the form of a man at the club who got up to get the paper his neighbor had refused to pass and fell down in the first stages of cholera, or of a shallowly buried corpse whose bones broke under his horse's hooves,[10] the signs of mortality surrounded him.

Sometimes all these pressures would build up intolerably, especially during those weeks or months when the rest of the family had already escaped to the hills, and he was left holding the fort in the heat. One such occasion is described as a "pivot" experience in his autobiography.

It happened one hot weather evening, in '86 or thereabouts, when I felt that I had come to the edge of all endurance. As I entered my empty house in the dusk there was no more in me except the horror of a great darkness, that I must have been fighting for some days. I came through that darkness alive, but how I do not know. (36:63–64)

How much was contributed to this horror by a disposition to depression inherited from his mother (Trix had more than one serious breakdown as she grew older), and how much by the years in Southsea, it is impossible to say. What is certain is that such an awareness of darkness, of an abyss, breaks through into Kipling's fiction at times, and that at others one senses a struggle (and an obligation to struggle) against its invading his work. Not for nothing did he give one of his earliest pieces of writing to be collected the title of a favorite discovery of his as an adolescent— James Thomson's *City of Dreadful Night*.

Early in 1884, Trix returned from England with her mother, and the Kiplings were reunited in what Alice Kipling used to refer to as the "Family Square." Rudyard had by now begun to master his trade and was being sent farther afield to cover important events elsewhere in India. Some of his articles even attracted the attention of the new viceroy, who within the year was also to discover what extraordinarily good company Alice Kipling could be, and indeed, how much more entertaining the whole Kipling family was than most of the Anglo-Indians on leave in the hill station of Simla. To the disgruntlement of many over whom they leapfrogged, the Kiplings had arrived. Small wonder, when the *Civil and Military* acquired a new editor who encouraged his gifted assistant to write topical fiction for the paper, that many of his early pieces were about Simla society.

In 1887 Kipling was transferred to the larger, parent newspaper, the *Pioneer*, in Allahabad, where one of his tasks was to edit a weekly magazine supplement, the *Week's News*, in which one of his own stories usually appeared. In 1888 his Lahore stories came out in book form as *Plain Tales from the Hills*, and most of the other stories he wrote in India were collected in subsequent volumes—paperbacks known as the Railway Series, designed to while away interminable train journeys in the Indian heat. Many, of course, accompanied such travelers all the way back to England in due course. So in a small way Kipling was preparing a wider public for the London debut he was by now actively contemplating. Even the money the books earned him was put aside to help pay his passage home. So when close friends of his, the Hills, decided to return to Mrs. Hill's home in Pennsylvania, Kipling was ready to accompany them and travel to England via the New World. And the *Pioneer* proved willing to help pay his way by commissioning a series of articles about the journey.[11]

Kipling's first visit to America, the country which was later to provide him with a wife and a home for four productive years, was not propitious. Greeted by reporters on his landing at San Francisco, he fired off a salvo of youthfully arrogant indiscretions which ensured that only the like were sought or remembered in future interviews. Similarily, his letters back to the *Pioneer*, unprotected by copyright, were gleefully and widely pirated (only the first of many such occasions) in an orgy of self-righteous indignation. An early one includes the following provocative passage.

When the City of Peking steamed through the Golden Gate, I saw with great joy that the blockhouse which guarded the mouth of "the finest harbor in the world, Sir," could be silenced by two gun boats from Hong Kong with safety, comfort, and despatch.[12]

As Angus Wilson points out, however, the series creates a very different impression if considered as a whole.

Yet discerning American readers must not only have admitted the justice of some of the criticism, but have seen (except perhaps in the sections on Chicago) that the young Englishman found much to like everywhere, and, more importantly, that in everything he wrote was a longing to love, a disposition to wonder and to admire, a hope that he would find here a freer and larger way of thinking about Anglo-Saxon civilization, a tougher more pioneering spirit united with the sort of easy culture that he found in his friend Mrs. Hill, a power of hard work, openness to risk, and acceptance of life's hardship which he feared (and he was right) he would not find when he got back to London.[13]

London

On arriving in London, Kipling found himself rooms in an unfashionable quarter, arranged for an English edition of the Railway Series, and began laying siege to magazine editors. Not that they put up much resistance. In London of the 1890s, full of art-for-art's-sake disciples of Wilde and Pater, the work of the brash young ex-Anglo-Indian was refreshingly different. He was hailed as the successor to Dickens, as an English Balzac, and in other such extravagant terms.[14] *The Times* itself wrote a glowing review of the whole Railway Series and expressed the hope that this gifted young author would have staying power, and not write himself out.

Of this there was little fear. Kipling soon learned to turn down editors as brusquely as he dismissed others who tried to lionize him. What angered him most was lavish praise of his aesthetic qualities from intellectuals whose languid way and view of life he despised—people totally out of sympathy with the values which his work extols, and which they had apparently not even noticed. Articles he was still sending back to the *Pioneer* began to adopt a self-consciously Philistine attitude, disparaging those around him who aired their knowledge of French writers whom, as we know from other sources, Kipling himself read and admired. As so often, we find him caught between two worlds and, as usual, seeming to prefer the world of action, even while continuing to function prolifically in that of the imagination.

For his first two years in England were amazingly productive. The poems he published in various magazines, and collected in *Barrack Room Ballads*, show a remarkable advance over the clever, gossipy *Departmental Ditties* he had published in India. And the stories he was writing about India, such as "On Greenhow Hill" and "Without Benefit of Clergy," were more ambitious and better than anything he had written before. At the same time, moreover, he was writing his first full-length novel, set not in India but in the London to which he had returned, and unlike anything else he wrote in being clearly autobiographical.

Productive it may have been, but this period in his life was also a very lonely one. A tentative affair with Caroline Taylor (Mrs. Hill's sister) had foundered on Kipling's less than orthodox religious beliefs. And a renewed acquaintance with a childhood sweetheart (whom he first met, incredibly, on a return visit to Southsea) also came to nothing. So he was ripe for human companionship when introduced, in 1890, to Wolcott Balestier, a young American acting as agent for an American publisher. The friendship flourished, and even led to their collaborating on an all-American romance set in India, *The Naulahka*. More important to Kipling in the long run, Wolcott's clever, strong-minded sister, Caroline, followed her brother to London to keep house for him. When Kipling first met her he was not the lonely figure of a year before, the whole family having returned from India on leave, and marriage was far from his thoughts. But Alice Kipling had no doubt, at first sight of this capable young woman just three years Kipling's senior, that she intended to marry her "Ruddy." And by 1891, when Kipling set out alone on doctor's orders for a trip round the world, something more than a merely friendly relationship had developed between them, though still no formal engagement.

Kipling never did get round the world, though he probably saw as much of it as he felt a need to at the time. His roots were still very much in India, as his writing was to attest for some years to come. And India had played a crucial role in shaping those increasingly unfashionable imperialist beliefs he was to hold till he died. For the minuscule and beleaguered Anglo-Indian community, which Kipling saw as perpetually threatened by, yet as constituting the only bulwark against, India's immense potential for cruelty and chaos, provided him with a powerful image of man's unending struggle to keep at bay the darkness and emptiness he knew to lie at the heart of things and of every individual.

That he should have seen this compassionate defense of order as so exclusively a *white* man's burden makes it much harder, though not impossible, for us to share his vision of India as symbolic of something far more universal.

Once having left India, however, Kipling came to realize more and more clearly that it was not a white man's country—that it must remain merely symbolic of a mission which, in practical terms, his Anglo-Saxon saviors of the world must achieve elsewhere. Indeed, in a work like *Kim* he could even rejoice in the intractable Indianness of India, and display a far deeper and more sympathetic understanding of the East than he is usually credited with. As for his idle and arrogant dream of settling Kashmir with British infantrymen— "and there they should breed us white soldiers, and perhaps a second fighting-line of Eurasians" (2:242)—it was no more than a dream. Increasingly his more realistic hopes for the future were based on the white dominions (including, of course, the biggest of all—the one that got away). So his aborted trip round the world can be seen as a kind of tour of inspection, with several weeks spent in South Africa, in Australia, and in New Zealand.

After New Zealand Kipling had intended a visit to R. L. Stevenson in Samoa, but something made him turn back and head for India. In Ceylon he heard from Caroline that Wolcott was seriously ill, and at Lahore, where his parents were once more in residence, news reached him of his friend's death. Without waiting even the few days till Christmas, he left for England, arriving there on January 10. And on January 18 he and Carrie were married.

America

The young couple set out on a prolonged, peripatetic honeymoon, calling on the bride's family in New England, and crossing the continent to sail for Japan from Vancouver. Here their wanderings were abruptly cut short when Kipling's bank closed its doors. Penniless, they were able to return to Carrie's family courtesy of Cooke's and Canadian Pacific, and there they remained, in Brattleboro, Vermont, for the next four years. Whether as a result of this incident or not, the family's finances were thereafter managed by the capable Carrie, as just one of the ways in which she undertook to protect her captive genius from all that might interfere with his work.

In Brattleboro, in a cottage belonging to Carrie's mother, they made their first home and had their first child, Josephine. But within the year (so quickly did the royalties come in and their fortunes mend) they were having a house built to their own design[15] on a plot leased for a nominal sum from Carrie's younger brother, Beatty. And there Kipling was soon at work on *The Jungle Books* and other Indian stories, including the first draft of what was to be his crowning (and only extended) masterpiece, *Kim*. From his immediate American environment he was perhaps too well sheltered by the new joys of marriage and fatherhood, and by the ever-protective Carrie; in any event, it had almost no impact on his writing. The only work of any note he wrote during this period which has an American setting is *Captains Courageous*. More revealing, in a curious way, about his feelings toward his new home is "An Error in the Fourth Dimension," a story about the impossibility of an American's settling in England and being accepted by his neighbors. Certainly what he and Carrie were trying to do, in snubbing neighbors and reporters alike, was something which, had he been writing the story instead of living it, he would have seen as bound to end in disaster. The resentment they incurred was exacerbated by tension between England and America over a border dispute between Venezuela and British Guiana, and came to a head in a quarrel with Carrie's brother.

Beatty, after welcoming the penniless Kiplings with characteristic warmth and generosity, had done well for himself financially by acting as Kipling's agent over building the house and other matters. But it irked him to be more and more dependent, as his other affairs failed to prosper, on his wealthy brother-in-law. And it irked him even more to be paid in small sums by a sister trying to exert control in this way over his extravagance. By all accounts his wife was even more outraged, especially when Carrie offered to look after her children if Beatty would move to an area where he could find steady employment. By the time he finally declared himself bankrupt, the whole town knew of the dispute, and most of course sided with good old generous-hearted Beatty. The climax of the quarrel was pure farce, with Beatty in a buggy dismounting Kipling on a bicycle, and in the course of an angry exchange threatening to kill him. Kipling put himself hopelessly in the wrong by preferring charges, and added insult to injury by offering to go bail for his brother-in-law. Life in Brattleboro, and indeed in America, became unthinkable, and it was Carrie's turn to be the exile in the land of her husband.

The Kiplings did return to America once more, in the winter of 1896–97. Carrie had a new baby son to show to her relatives, and winter in England proved too wet for all of them. But they were greeted in New York by a threatened lawsuit from Beatty, and added to that the two older children and Rudyard were desperately ill within days of their arrival. For a week or more Kipling's life hung in the balance, and during this time his eldest and "best beloved" daughter died. As during her brother's final illness, Carrie took charge, at whatever cost, coping not only with floods of sympathetic letters and telegrams from all over the world, and the constant siege of newspaper reporters, but with yet another unpleasant case of a publisher's pirating Kipling's work. Small wonder this was their last visit to the United States.

As in so many love-hate relationships, Kipling loved America for what he wanted her to be, and hated her for not being what he wanted her to be. Of all the Americans he met, the one he liked and admired the most, apart from his wife, was Theodore Roosevelt, with whom he kept up a lifelong correspondence. For he possessed what Kipling had known in the best of the Anglo-Indians, and was to find in Cecil Rhodes and Lord Milner: the toughness, the confidence, the conviction of self-worth needed to establish the paternalistic, white, Anglo-Saxon hegemony Kipling saw as necessary to keep at bay the encroaching chaos. It was to Roosevelt, of course, at the time of America's war with Spain and the annexing of Cuba and the Phillipines, that he addressed his poem "The White Man's Burden."

Perhaps the American of whom Kipling retained the most negative memory was the child of rich parents aboard the ship that first brought him to America.

This spoiled boy, out of control, noisy, pert, blasé was almost everything that was blasphemy to Kipling's concept of childhood as a wonder time, with a vision of its own that transcends the grown man's. It is a measure of his love for children that he should have saved that vile child up in his mind not to punish him but to redeem him six years later in *Captains Courageous*.[16]

The irony, of course, is that the description is not far from the one Mrs. Holloway might have given of Kipling as a boy.

England and South Africa

By the time Kipling left America, only *Kim* remained to be completed of his Indian stories. No longer could he postpone the business of putting down fresh roots. He was not quite thirty, and the process should not have been unduly difficult. Yet new roots for the artist are notoriously tender growths. The names are legion of authors—whether James Joyce or George Eliot or Willa Cather—in whose work only the ambience of their most formative years is ever wholly recaptured. In Kipling's case, of course, many of these were spent in no-man's-land, and the India of his early childhood and early manhood is his first home and real love. But the basic, unspoken premise of an Anglo-Indian's whole attitude to life was that everything must be regarded as provisional—that he did not really belong where he felt most at home. (It is significant that, after leaving India in 1889, Kipling returned only once, for the briefest of visits.) Perhaps Kipling is a premature instance of that modern phenomenon, the rootless man. That he did in fact succeed in striking new attachments of a kind is clear from much of his subsequent writing, but what is often equally apparent is how hard he had to try.

First of the factors that helped him feel at home was that he was no longer a seven-days' wonder, the *enfant terrible* of the right, in English letters. Rather, he had become a member of the establishment, elected as the youngest member of its holy of holies, the Athenaeum Club. The columns of *The Times* were open to him at will, and when, in the year of the Golden Jubilee, he sent them what has become one of his best-known poems, "Recessional," he was widely regarded as a sort of unofficial poet laureate. He dined at the High Table of Balliol College, Oxford, and was given a standing ovation by the students. All this at thirty!

Second, he became a regular guest aboard flagships at naval maneuvers, and turned to writing stories about the fleet rather than the army, Pyecroft displacing Mulvaney. If they are less successful, this is partly because Kipling's firsthand knowledge of the navy was derived so exclusively from the bridge and the officers' mess. In this as in most spheres, he was losing that common touch which had given *Barrack Room Ballads* and the Mulvaney stories their unique quality.

Third, after a disastrous first winter near Torquay, the family found a comfortable home near Rottingdean, within easy reach of friends and relatives. Five years later the combination of too many curious holidaymakers from nearby Brighton, and too many memories of Josephine's few happy years in England, drove Kipling to "Bateman's," a Jacobean mansion deep in rural Sussex. But he had by this time developed a passion for motoring, and continued his discovery of the English countryside from this new base.

Yet still there was the urge to wander. And still the wet winters troubled them. In 1898 the Kiplings took to spending a few months of every year in South Africa, and here Kipling's imperialism became much more strident, before suffering its severest setback. Here he met men like Lord Milner, the governor general, and Cecil Rhodes, founding father of Rhodesia. The latter even built them a house, "The Woolsack," on his estate and made it available to the Kiplings for as many English winters as they chose. In them he seems to have found the Old World equivalent of Teddy Roosevelt—men equal to assuming the white man's burden. He met them, moreover, as equals, sharing their dreams for the future of South Africa, a land whose climate would allow the white man to take permanent possession in pursuit of his civilizing mission. Unfortunately for the British, however, Dutch settlers had arrived there first, and come to regard it as their homeland. Deeply and conservatively religious, and committed to a patriarchally rural way of life, they resented the gradual take-over of the country by the much more commercially minded British. They tried to escape to the interior and start over again, but the expansionist aims of men like Rhodes made it inevitable that, sooner or later, they would have to stand their ground and fight.

During the Boer War itself, Kipling threw himself into helping to edit a newspaper for the troops, raised a quarter of a million for tobacco and other comforts from the royalties on a popular song, and obviously hugely enjoyed the status all this gave him. Less attractively, his accounts of the fighting have the same kind of adolescent enthusiasm as the worst of his Indian stories. And he is insistently and insensitively critical of British attempts not to wage war on the civilian population—a policy which naturally allowed the citizen army they were fighting to slip in and out of protected civilian status at will.

To give Kipling his due, he saw the Boers as neither capable of nor interested in building his kind of brave new world, as Rhodes was busy doing on experimental fruit farms which were to contribute so much to South Africa's prosperity, and which did so much to raise the standard of living and the expectations of the native workers. Prophetically, moreover, he recognized their exercise of a God-given authority over the Africans as far more repressive and inflexibly exploitive than Rhodes's liberal paternalism. Thus of the attempt, after the eventual British victory, to win over the Boers by relatively generous peace-treaty terms he could write: "We put them in a position to uphold and expand their primitive lust for racial domination, and thanked God we were 'rid of a knave'" (36:159).

His anger at the British government, and even Lord Milner, for what he regarded as a betrayal of the imperialist vision, was typical of the idealist uninvolved in the day-to-day realities of practical policy. But it also indicates that Kipling, a visitor for a few short months a year, and moving within a rarefied circle of highly placed friends, never came to know South Africans of any race at all well. As a young man in India, he had been able to believe ardently in the British mission there, yet in many instances to write with greater affection and understanding of Indians than of the British. There was always a part of Kipling that did not want the British to change the India he came to know and love—that was glad, almost, that the task was probably beyond them. In none of the few stories he wrote with a South African background is there any comparably fruitful tension or ambivalence. He had become the prisoner of a theoretical imperialism, and no longer felt its reality.

Home at Last

"The Woolsack," to which Kipling never returned after 1908, was his last real *pied-à-terre* outside Britain, though as the German menace increased he felt himself drawn closer and closer to France, which both before and after the war became a kind of second home. It seems that this most xenophobic of English authors could only maintain his ardor by being, for at least part of the year, an expatriate. "What should they know of England," he had once written, "who only England know?"[17]

A more pertinent question in Kipling's case, however, might be: "What should they know who know everywhere but England of those who know nowhere but England?" For the years between the Boer War and the Great War are perhaps the saddest in Kipling's life to have to recall. It was a period of increasing and embittered isolation when fewer and fewer people shared Kipling's imperial dream, and when he was prepared to consider fewer and fewer viewpoints which did not coincide with his own. Of a particularly savage attack on the government in 1914, in which he described plans to give home rule to Ireland as a betrayal of Ulster to a gang of criminals, Lord Birkenhead writes that "This crazy outburst marked the lowest point yet reached by Kipling's sagging reputation."[18]

This alienation from his fellow countrymen applied to both ends of the social spectrum. In many ways this was nothing new as far as the upper echelons of society were concerned. In their company, despite his reverence for authority, Kipling had always felt, and often been regarded as, an outsider. His respect was reserved too exclusively for competence and efficiency of the kind he admired in any master of his trade, whether a ship's engineer, a builder of bridges, or a district commissioner keeping the peace between warring tribes on the North West Frontier. So, not surprisingly, he despised the ruling classes' God-given right to a cherished and usually incompetent amateurism. He was particularly critical, for instance, when rank-and-file soldiers died during the Boer War as a result of blunders, whether by generals or politicans, which were all too reminiscent of the charge of the Light Brigade. In later years, the continued refusal of those in high places to recognize in Germany the menace Kipling so prophetically discerned alienated him more and more from the easygoing establishment of the Conservative party, including his cousin Stanley Baldwin. His political allies came to be drawn from nearer and nearer to what was considered a lunatic fringe.

This drift to the right was reinforced by Kipling's equal disenchantment with the other end of the social scale. As prospective emigrants to Canada, South Africa, Australia, and New Zealand, or as troops to fight the Afghans, the Boers, and the Germans, Kipling trusted the rank and file more than their leaders. But as miners striking for higher wages, as voters electing a Liberal government which offered them some measure of social justice, or as Irishmen desirous of ruling themselves, the newly enfranchised lower orders forfeited all Kipling's sympathies.

It was the formative influence of India which at a conscious level, doubtless, left Kipling with such a distrust of democracy. India was so ungovernable, in his view, that only the "strong man governing alone" could impose law and any semblance of order on its multitude of competing races, religions, sects, creeds, and castes. So Yardley-Orde on the frontier is a fictional forerunner of such other admired governors of the ungovernable as Teddy Roosevelt in America, Milner in South Africa—and, eventually, Mussolini in Italy. Even Britain herself was becoming less and less governable. Yet, as already suggested, Kipling's reverence for the law, and for authority strong enough to preserve it, together with his almost pathological fear of chaos, may well have been a legacy of something far deeper and more private in his makeup. Bruno Bettelheim records how those who survived in Nazi death camps for anything approaching Kipling's five and a half years in the House of Desolation frequently did so at the cost of identifying to an increasing extent with their perse-cutors.[19] It is not fanciful, I suggest, to assume that Kipling as a child came to accept many of Mrs. Holloway's strictures as to some extent deserved, and that later in life he projected the suppressed guilt at his own unruliness on to others around him at the same time as, self-protectively, he took sides with authority.

Be that as it may, Kipling's political fantasies and parables from this period, such as "The Army of a Dream" (1904) and "The Mother Hive" (1908), are among the least attractive of his writings. Fortunately these years were also a time when Kipling was learning to incorporate a sense of the English landscape, and in many cases of the history that landscape embodies, into his stories. This is most obviously true of *Puck of Pook's Hill* and *Rewards and Fairies* but also applies to a story like "They" (1904), the first piece of writing in which Kipling allows himself to acknowledge his grief at the death of Josephine, five years earlier.

Just eleven years later, in 1915, John Kipling was killed barely six weeks after landing in France, fighting in a war his father had so presciently warned his fellow countrymen about. Prior to this Kipling had visited the troops at the front, pulled strings to get his nearsighted seventeen-year-old son a commission in the Irish Guards, and written three stories which are profoundly disturb-ing studies of hatred—brilliantly so in the case of "Mary Post-gate." After his son's death, Kipling withdrew deep within his shell till long after the armistice, devoting himself to an extended and painful labor of love in the form of an official history of *The Irish Guards in the Great War*.

Kipling's attitude to official recognition was, throughout his life, strongly idiosyncratic. He was seriously considered for the position of poet laureate, after the death of Tennyson, in 1892, but refused to let his name go forward. Twice, in 1899 and 1903, he turned down offers of knighthoods of increasing seniority, which is perhaps understandable in view of some of the company he would have been keeping. But even attempts to make him a Companion of Honor in 1917, and to bestow the Order of Merit on him in 1921 and again 1924, failed, though both of these are much more exclusive orders reserved for those of truly outstanding achievement. Winston Churchill, T. S. Eliot, and Bertrand Russell all held the Order of Merit—and, coincidentally or not, all were subsequently awarded the Nobel Prize for Literature, as was Kipling in 1907. Similarly he received honorary doctorates from the universities of Durham, Oxford, and McGill. It was only official recognition by the state, it seems, which he felt might compromise him.

Kipling's later life was plagued by illness. From 1915 onward he suffered intermittently from severe gastritis, which was finally diagnosed as an ulcer but which for years he feared was cancer. Hence the number of instances of cancer in his later work. Coming after his son's death, this constant threat seems to have given rise to a remarkable series of stories in his last two major collections on such themes as illness, suffering, self-sacrifice, healing, and forgiveness. This is not to say that the postwar Kipling did not continue to be a crusty old reactionary, out of tune with the times, and to publish things from time to time which reflected this. But he was no longer active politically and no longer a public figure. He was able to travel widely, on behalf of the War Graves Commission, on visits to his diplomat son-in-law, and on pure pleasure trips, without being besieged by the local press. And as he withdrew more and more from the limelight, the best of his stories, themselves attracting much less attention, show a relaxed mellowness and explore new, more subtle, less strident themes than those of his middle period.

His death in 1936, a month after his seventieth birthday, passed almost unnoticed by a press and a public anxiously awaiting news of the dying King George V.

Chapter Two
The Indian Stories

Kipling was still a boy at the time he returned to India. As a result, when he began writing stories for publication he had no adult experience to draw on which was not Indian. His readership, moreover, was exclusively Anglo-Indian, and his training as a writer for the previous two or three years had been as a reporter and close observer of the Indian scene. Not surprisingly, therefore, the stories he wrote for the remainder of his time in India were about India. Even after his return to London, what established his reputation in the first place was the reissue in England of what he had already published in India, and what continued to hold his readers' interest was more stories about India, with their intriguing blend of a highly exotic setting and extreme, down-to-earth realism of incident and language. Not until toward the end of his time in America did he begin to write fewer Indian than non-Indian stories, though it is interesting to note that the two *Jungle Books* and *Kim*, written for and/or about children, account for much of his later Indian output. Nor is this the only sign that his view of India was becoming increasingly nostalgic.

The broad thematic categories into which Kipling's Indian stories for adults most naturally fall are (1) those about Anglo-Indian life; (2) those about the Indian army, and in particular about privates Mulvaney, Learoyd, and Orthoris; (3) those about native Indian life. Obviously the categories overlap. Stories about officer life in the army are often barely distinguishable from those about civilian Anglo-Indian life, since members of the two groups came from more or less the same social class. Kipling's great breakthrough, in his military stories, was to write about private soldiers—a species almost as exotic and unknown to some of his readers in England as Pathans and Bengalis. Then there are stories in which interest is more or less equally divided between Indian and Anglo-Indian characters—some of them among the best he ever wrote. Nevertheless, the broad categories still hold sufficiently to be a useful way of examining the stories in more detail.

Anglo-Indian Stories

Of the twenty-one stories first published in 1887 and subsequently collected in book form, fifteen deal with Anglo-Indian life, as do nineteen of the forty-nine first published in 1888. The action of almost all of them, moreover, takes place in the hill station of Simla, where most of the characters we meet are on summer leave rather than engaged in their day-to-day occupations. Partly for this reason, and partly also because the population of Simla in the summer included such an abnormally high concentration of Anglo-Indians, almost none of the stories so much as refers to an Indian character. But most importantly of all, of course, the great majority first appeared in the *Civil and Military Gazette* or the *Pioneer*, so they were written to fill a particular need (and even a given space on the page) for a particular audience, who were much more interested in reading about themselves than about any damned natives.

So we read about older, wiser women rescuing foolish young men ("The Rescue of Pluffles," "Kidnapped") and pretty young women rescuing themselves ("Cupid's Arrows," "Wressley of the Foreign Office") from unfortunate attachments or suitors; about the misunderstandings and misadventures of unsuccessful ("Bitters Neat," "On the Strength of a Likeness") and successful ("Miss Youghal's Sais," "False Dawn") courtship; about marriages that fail ("The Other Man," "Watches of the Night") and succeed ("Yoked with an Unbeliever," "Three and —an Extra"); about newcomers who fail to adapt to Indian life and earn our pity ("Thrown Away") or contempt ("A Bank Fraud"); and so on. As a group, such stories are almost exclusively concerned with social situations, conventions, rituals, and games within an exclusively European society. In a word, they are tribal stories, reflecting such tribal values as a mistrust of all intellectuals ("The Conversion of Aurelian McGoggin," "Wressley of the Foreign Office"), emphasizing the perils of cutting oneself off from the tribe ("By Word of Mouth"), and gleefully recounting the elaborate vengeance of the tribe on the outsider or offender ("A Friend's Friend").

Once we grasp this tribal quality, we shall better understand the tone employed in so many of the stories by the narrator—a knowing, dogmatic tone which clearly relishes enunciating those pearls of tribal wisdom which are sure to elicit nods of sage approval. Here, for instance, is the twenty-year-old Kipling delivering himself rather pompously on the subject of love and marriage in the opening sentences of three of the stories.

After marriage arrives a reaction, sometimes a big, sometimes a little one; but it comes sooner or later, and must be tidied over by both partners if they desire the rest of their lives to go with the current.

The oldest trouble in the world comes from want of understanding. And it is entirely the fault of the woman. Somehow, she is built incapable of speaking the truth, even to herself. She only finds it out about four months later, when the man is dead, or has been transferred. Then she says she never was so happy in her life, and marries someone else....

We are a high-caste and enlightened race, and infant-marriage is very shocking and the consequences are sometimes peculiar; but, nevertheless, the Hindu notion—which is the Continental notion, which is the aboriginal notion—of arranging marriages irrespective of the personal inclinations of the married, is sound.... How can a man...who cannot be trusted to pick up at sight a moderately sound horse...go about the choosing of a wife?[1]

But is it Kipling speaking? Are we justified in assuming that author and narrator are identical? A somewhat similar, and rather irritating, knowing tone is admittedly to be found in Kipling's later work, particularly in his more didactic verse. But it is so extraordinarily pervasive in these early stories that we must view it, I think, as a feature of the genre he devises, along with hints now and then that he is writing *contes à clef*, and frequent willful digressions concluding in the catch phrase, "But that is another story." For Kipling is writing not only for a known readership but a readership in the know—or one that liked to be treated as if it were, and to find its knowledgeability so faithfully mirrored in such liberally scattered nuggets of prejudice.

For us, however, who are at half a world and a century's remove, this catering to the views of the society for which Kipling is writing becomes a part of his description of the society about which he is writing, since they are one and the same. And for selected readers of his own day, who must have been aware at times of a certain ironic distance between Kipling and his narrator, the same would have been true. In the lengthy introduction to "The Conversion of Aurelian McGoggin," for instance, we find complacency as to the broad-minded tolerance of those who are clearly rather petty and intolerant; we encounter disingenuous antiintellectualism; we recognize the broadest tongue-in-cheek flattery of those educated in the Indian school of hard knocks and harsh realities; and finally we detect irony verging on sarcasm.

Life, in India, is not long enough to waste in proving that there is no one in particular at the head of affairs. For this reason. The Deputy is above the Assistant, the Commissioner above the Deputy, the Lieutenant-Governor above the Commissioner, the Viceroy above all four, under the orders of the Secretary of State who is responsible to the Empress. If the Empress be not responsible to her Maker—if there is no Maker for her to be responsible to—the entire system of Our administration must be wrong. Which is manifestly impossible. (1:127–28)

Many of his readers tended to see things the other way around, of course, regarding the British Empire as more than ample proof of the existence of God. So, without giving them time to realize that the tables have been turned, and the whole rationale for the British presence in India playfully called in question, Kipling concludes the paragraph with a comforting reaffirmation of the supremacy of what matters over mind. Yet those who saw no irony, who merely nodded sagely, were not being cheated by the author. For, at the same time as he himself seems to have had no particular belief in anyone "in particular at the head of affairs," he believed strongly in the desirability of people's believing in something (just what did not much matter) which would give them a code by which and a structure within which to live. Far from being simplistically orthodox, therefore, these early stories contain surprising, even if still rather crudely executed, complexities.

The stories themselves, written in haste and necessarily too short for any real development to take place, are for the most part neatly turned but rather shallow tales—after dinner literature, to be read over a cigar before joining the ladies. Yet by their sheer economy, and their ability to capture a situation, together with the salient features of the characters involved, in just a handful of pages, they illustrate how Kipling's apprenticeship as a journalist was preparing him to be the outstanding writer of short stories he was to become, and probably saving him from dwindling into the third-rate novelist he might otherwise have been. Moreover, in many ways these unpretentious jottings from a kind of weekly gossip column give a more reliable guide to at least certain aspects of Anglo-Indian life than the more consciously crafted stories written after Kipling's return to England. In these latter we have a sense that Kipling is reassessing his response to Anglo-India in the light of his disappointment with the shiftlessness and lack of purpose or nerve which he finds in England.

This is very obvious in the rather crudely polemic "Head of the District" (1893). The story begins movingly with Yardley-Orde, deputy commissioner of a troubled frontier district, on his way back to the plains in a high fever and a litter. He is held up by the flooded Indus and dies before his wife can be ferried across to join him. The rest of the story turns on the appointment of an Indian to succeed Orde as head of the district—supposedly the kind of idiotic gesture by which a central government under pressure from "enlightened" elements in Britain was all too fond of undermining the best efforts of those on the spot, those in a position to "know." The Indian in question, a university-educated Bengali (i.e., a plainsman, and a Hindu to boot), is, of course, ludicrously unequal to the task of controlling the feuding frontier tribes he is to govern. Orde's assistant, Tallentyre (the man who ought obviously to have been put in charge), barely keeps the tribesmen's rebellious outrage within bounds at having a "black

Bengali dog" sent to rule them, but does manage to return the new deputy commissioner to safety. The latter's brother, however, loses his head in a panic-stricken flight in the wrong direction. (The head is later returned to Tallentyre with the comment: "See, no man kept the spectacles, though they were of gold.")

In fact, of course, no central goverment, however misguided, ever made such a totally inappropriate appointment. But the story serves to bring into sharp and rather unpleasant focus a feature of Kipling's attitude to Indians. For "the real native," as he describes him elsewhere, he has genuine liking and respect. But for the "hybrid, University-trained mule" (2:225) he has nothing but contempt. (T. E. Lawrence much preferred Bedouins to Damascus city Arabs; North Americans have been known to feel that *their* Indians belong in camp rather than on campus. Are we merely anxious to preserve our own privileged status, or do we in fact dislike being thus confronted by our own image, as parents sometimes dislike having to recognize their faults in their children?) Most distasteful of all, Kipling taunts his poor miscast Bengali with "fearing physical pain as some men fear sin," and contrasts this in almost adolescent glee with the single-minded barbarity of the tribesmen who murder his brother.

"William the Conqueror," a much more "acceptable" version of the indispensability of the British in India, was written during Kipling's stay in America, for the *Ladies' Home Journal.* It tells of a love affair that flourishes during a mission of mercy to a famine-stricken area of South India, and is Kipling's one direct confrontation with this recurring grim reality in Indian life. Because the protagonists, though sincere and devoted, are above it all, however, returning at the end to a more fertile north, we do not feel the menace as we do that of cholera in "Without Benefit of Clergy." The story is also one of Kipling's few excursions into the vast peninsula to the south of the mountains and fertile plains he knew so well. And in its account of the return to the Punjab, we sense just how much Kipling felt this to be a homecoming. The boyish, self-reliant heroine was probably his tribute to the American girl as he saw her.

Written somewhat earlier in England, "At the End of the
Passage" presents the same basic thesis through the lives of four
isolated, selflessly devoted administrators who ride hundreds of
miles each week for a game of bridge in each other's company.
Yet Kipling's vision here is also very nearly of something more—
something quite different. For the combined effects of prolonged
loneliness, of overwork, of heat, and of sleeplessness build up
frighteningly so as to precipitate a horrifying climax to the story.
Read in conjunction with a few other such scattered glimpses in
Kipling's work of the horror, the darkness, the abyss over which
we all pirouette or plod, the story allows us to speculate, in
passing, about the kind of writer Kipling avoided being, and the
kind he did not aspire to be. It has just enough of Conrad in it, and
little enough of Somerset Maugham, to let us see more clearly
what Kipling achieved, and what he chose not to attempt.

Far the richest and most complex of these stories in praise of
the British role in India is "The Bridge-Builders." It is one of
Kipling's last few Indian stories, and one in which Anglo-Indian
and native elements are of more or less equal importance.
Recounting the building of a bridge over the Ganges, and its
withstanding a sudden and awesome flood just weeks before its
completion, the story is also an excellent example of a genre
which was becoming increasingly important in Kipling's work: a
celebration of the high and often heroic skills of the modern
technological craftsman-artist. The opening pages take us into
the world of Findlayson, the engineer who designed the bridge, of
his assistant, young Hitchcock, and of Peroo, the lascar seaman
turned foreman of the tacklemen who perform the difficult, high
girder work. Kipling pays his tribute by immersing himself and
us in the thought processes and vocabulary of men whose lives
have for three years virtually consisted of building a bridge. This
identification is the easier and more convincing because for
Kipling the act of writing has equally, by this stage in his career,
become a craft carried to the point of passion.

Word comes that flood waters are on their way down from the
Ganges's headwaters; these arrive earlier than forecast; and, in
the strain and confusion of making fast everything that could

break loose and endanger the bridge, Findlayson swallows two or
three of the opium pellets that Peroo offers him to stave off
encroaching weariness. When some of the boats for carrying
stone break free under the impact of a floating tree, Findlayson
applies himself to solving the problem, and Kipling captures his
opium-induced state of mind in the engineering terms in which
Findlayson continues to think.

An immensely complex plan had suddenly flashed into Findlayson's
mind. He saw the ropes running from boat to boat in straight lines and
angles—each rope a line of white fire. But there was one rope which was
the master rope. He could see that rope. If he could pull it once, it was
absolutely and mathematically certain that the disordered fleet would
reassemble itself in the backwater behind the guard-tower. (13:28)

Accompanied by the faithful Peroo, Findlayson is swept down-
stream in one of the boats he tries to recapture, and for the rest of
the story we eavesdrop on a conversation among what we at first
assume to be the motley collection of animals and men taking
refuge on the same island as the two bridge-builders, and trans-
mogrified by the opium into the gods of Hinduism. They have
assembled to hear Gunga or mother Ganges's complaint against
the indignity of a bridge spanning her waters whose destruction
she finds she cannot achieve, unaided. She recruits an ally in Kali
(goddess of death and destruction), but most of the others argue
that the white man and his trains have increased the number of
pilgrims visiting their shrines, and have even speeded up the
spread of disease, which should please Kali. The white man's
gods, moreover, are no threat, since they are so easily converted
into such Indian equivalents as Mary carved with twelve arms.
Finally, any work of man is so temporary as not to be worth the
gods' anger. "Let the dirt dig in the dirt ere it return to the dirt,"
says Ganesh (who, as patron of all practical enterprises, is presumably partial to bridges). And many readers have taken the
function of this second half of the story to be to place the
transient works of man in the perspective of eternity.[2] This,

however, is to leave one of Kipling's most interesting and revealing stories at the level of cliché or truism.

For the most important part of the conversation takes place when the late comer, Krishna (god of love), warns his fellow deities that the real threat comes from neither bridges nor the white man's gods, but from ideas, which they cannot now hope to defeat.

"It is too late now. Ye should have slain at the beginning when the men from across the water had taught our folk nothing. Now my people see their work, and go away thinking. They do not think of the Heavenly Ones altogether. They think of the fire-carriage and the other things that the bridge-builders have done, and when your priests thrust forward hands asking alms, they give a little unwillingly. That is the beginning, among one or two, or five or ten—for I, moving among my people, know what is in their hearts." (13:47)

The other gods ridicule the idea that this is the beginning of any kind of end, or uneasily console themselves with the thought that "It is very far away," and Indra (god of war) reassures them that only "when Brahm ceases to dream, the Heavens and Hells and Earth disappear. Be content. Brahm dreams still" (13:50). But in the morning, when the flood is subsiding and the two men find themselves alone on the island, Peroo discovers that Findlayson has shared his dream of "the island ... full of beasts and men talking." His immediate response is:

"Oho! Then it *is* true. 'When Brahm ceases to dream, the Gods die.' Now I know, indeed, what he meant. Once, too, the *guru* said as much; but then I did not understand. Now I am wise." (13:53)

So far from surveying men's actions from the point of view of the gods, therefore, the story looks at the gods from the point of view of man and his growing powers—not arrogantly, for man and his works are as temporary as ever, but sadly, since they too must pass, and sooner even than man. As Peroo perceives, it is the gods who die when man awakens.[3]

"The Bridge-Builders" is probably Kipling's most convincing presentation of his tenaciously held belief in the divine right of the British to save India from itself. This is partly because the Englishmen in question are technicians, solving purely technical problems, but also because Kipling sets their efforts against a vision of an India which, while benefiting from their labors, subsumes them within an enduring reality which remains essentially Indian. Yet, if that were all, the story might still seem merely a piece of nineteenth-century materialistic arrogance. India, however, is so vast and the changes wrought by man so puny that it readily becomes a metaphor for the human condition. It represents the physical universe of time and space, the chaos of flood and famine and disease, the whirlpool eddying around a death beyond which there are no gods—the environment within which man must build bridges and dams and hospitals (and sing songs and tell stories and learn to watch his loved ones die), knowing there may be nothing else. The abyss is just as real as that in "At the End of the Passage," but Kipling's emphasis here is on the importance of ignoring or forgetting its existence by immersing oneself not in the opiate but rather in the challenge and the fascination of work.

Military Stories

If the best of Kipling's Anglo-Indian stories are also Indian, and vice versa—if, in fact, the stoutest of these seedlings, despite Kipling's avowed dislike of such, are hybrids—the same cannot be said of his military tales. For the hallmark of the most memorable of these—the ones about privates Mulvaney, Learoyd, and Orthoris—is the self-sufficing, claustrophobic quality of the life led in garrison or barracks. Mulvaney's relationships with native Indians, when not conducted at bayonet point, are minimal, and those with officers and (with few exceptions) civilians strictly professional and prescribed. Each of the stories has a frame, in that it is told by one or more of these three inseparables to a Kipling-like narrator who is far more self-effacing than his equivalent in the early Anglo-Indian stories. And each concerns the deeds and misdeeds, long past or recent, of one or more of the trio. Thus in a dozen and a half stories the three characters and their relationships, and the format, are established as nowhere else in Kipling's work.

Naturally the stories are of uneven quality. Some of the early ones, such as "Private Learoyd's Story," "The Incarnation of Krishna Mulvaney," and above all "The Three Musketeers," are just good fun—farcical accounts of practical jokes such as Kipling enjoyed writing all his life, and not unlike the schoolboy stories in *Stalky & Co.* Equally immature in tone, but unpleasantly so, "With the Main Guard" describes hand-to-hand fighting on the frontier at great length and with evident relish. "I say there's nothin' better than the bay'nit, wid a long reach, a double twist av ye can, an' a slow recover," says Mulvaney, with all that loving concern that so many of Kipling's protagonists show for the precise skills of their trade. And then, acknowledging that the other two approach matters differently: "Each does ut his own way, like makin' love..., the butt or the bay'nit or the bullet accordin' to the natur' av the man" (2:159). As if sensing he may have offended some readers, however, Kipling closes the story with his three musketeers coming off guard to find the two-year-old daughter of the sergeant wandering sleepless around the barracks, and has them return her to her quarters. But a dash of sentimentality at the last minute cannot disguise the flavor the story as a whole leaves in the mouth. Its one redeeming, memorable feature is that it is told by Mulvaney to distract Learoyd and help him through a long Indian night when the heat threatens to drive him to suicide. We are given another glimpse of the abyss.

Most of a soldier's time, however, is not spent fighting, and most of Kipling's stories are concerned with boredom, and the relief of boredom, in camp or barracks. Of the later, more somber stories on this theme, "Love-O'-Women" is chiefly memorable for its frame, and in particular its superb opening paragraph. By contrast, "The Courting of Dinah Shadd"—which is recounted while on maneuvers rather than in barracks—suffers from a frame which, though clever, is too long, and does little to enhance what might otherwise be the most moving of all Mulvaney's yarns. He recalls his courtship, and how by incredible foolishness, the very night Dinah promises to be his, he brings on his own head and that of whoever shall marry him a drunken old Irish-woman's curse. He also recalls with increasing bitterness how, since then, by periodic foolishness and an incurable thirst, he has helped fulfill her prophecy.

Mulvaney speaks in what passes for a broad Irish brogue; Learoyd and Orthoris use what more often fail to pass for York-shire and Cockney accents, respectively. There is usually some-thing condescending about an author's using dialect so exten-sively, and Mulvaney's brogue helps to prevent his becoming more than one of what Kipling elsewhere describes as "that quaint, crooked, sweet, profoundly irresponsible and profoundly lovable race that fight like fiends, argue like children, reason like women and obey like men."[4] Nevertheless, Mulvaney is an exam-ple, indeed one of the most notable examples, of how Kipling's feeling for character and his gift for transmitting character depend on his acute ear for the kind of language men use, and on his powers of written mimicry. Nor should it be forgotten that the clipped, cliché-ridden speech of Kipling's Anglo-Indians, or of the subalterns (i.e., lieutenants and second lieutenants) recounting their hair-raising and horrific experiences during the Burma campaign in "A Conference of the Powers," is no less a dialect than Mulvaney's, and no less indicative of racial and individual character.

In any case, in this particular story the women characters ensure that the brogue in which it is told carries with it no note of condescension. There is first the fearsomely pathetic figure of Mother Sheehy uttering her curse, and second the frail dignity of the young Dinah (whose "thin ... hand dhropped into mine like a rose-leaf into a muddy road") as she says: "The half av that I'll take ..., an' more too if I can. Go home, ye silly talking' woman—go home an' confess." These two hoist the story from the level of caricature to something Synge might not have been overly ashamed to have written. We do not feel it more than fleetingly ridiculous that the narrator should wake, at the end of the story, to see "Mulvaney, the night dew gemming his moustache, leaning on his rifle at picket, lonely as Prometheus on his rock, with I know not what vultures tearing his liver."

A more complete success, artistically, is Private Learoyd's one tour de force in "On Greenhow Hill." The frame here is the perfect foil. The regiment is under canvas, and a deserter from the native regiment accompanying them has been disturbing their sleep by sniping and trying to encourage others to join him and his tribesmen friends. So the three musketeers have chosen a vantage point the next day, and are passing the time till marksman Orthoris can get a shot at the deserter as he comes up the valley for his next night's work. Learoyd speculates that the desertion was probably "for th' sake of a lass," and recalls the lass who, conversely, was responsible for his enlisting. The not very gentle giant then goes on to recount, haltingly, how he fell and lay unconscious all night after a drinking bout, how he woke to find he had broken his arm and was being cared for by a nearby Methodist household, how with many a struggle and some backsliding he came more and more under their gentle spell and especially that of the daughter, how he nearly killed the preacher he thought was his rival till he learned she was dying of consumption and was for no man, and how her approaching death drove him to enlist. And every now and then, as the story unfolds, we are reminded by some movement or comment from Orthoris of the reason for their being there. Obviously the two stories reach their conclusions almost simultaneously. One of them is as casually and as mindlessly brutal as anything in Kipling. Yet, juxtaposed to the almost grotesque tenderness of Learoyd's story, the violence is far from gratuitous.

Perhaps the masterpiece of these stories, however, is the slightly earlier "Black Jack," just because it so economically uses nothing but the boredom and tensions of life in barracks as its raw material. Mulvaney has been unfairly charged by a sergeant still wet behind the ears with being dirty on parade, and fairly charged with insulting him as a result. He recounts, with a shudder, how near he came to killing the offender when taunted by him while doing his three-hour punishment pack drill. Then he recalls an earlier injustice when he was much younger, the

offending sergeant much older, and when for the honor of the
regiment he had contrived to save the latter from a richly
deserved death at the hands of a bunch of raw recruits. What was
more, having refused to join their conspiracy, he had to outwit
the plan he overheard them hatching to let him take the blame
for the sergeant's death, yet not let anyone suspect he knew of
such a plan.

On its own, Mulvaney's yarn would be a well-told one of
intrigue and excitement. It is the interaction between frame and
story, teller and tale, that makes it something more.[5] Everything
in the earlier story was so much larger than life as Mulvaney now
lives it. The sergeant was so much blacker a villain—a womanizer
as well as a bully—yet a man who, when faced with death, earned
Mulvaney's grudging respect. Moreover, instead of being goaded
almost to the point of killing him, Mulvaney risked his life to save
him. Those were days when he still had hopes of wearing stripes
himself. So much older now, and so much wiser about himself in
so many ways, Mulvaney looks back at a younger man in so many
ways his superior.

The lives Kipling's soldiers lead are even more claustrophobi-
cally circumscribed than those of his Anglo-Indians. Yet they
exhibit a richness and a variety of emotional response not found
in the latter. This is partly the result of Kipling's choosing to
make his central character an Irishman—a member of a race he
felt strongly drawn to, envied, and despised all his days for the
way they seemed to him to be able to evade the burdens and
responsibilities of adulthood and Anglo-Saxonhood. It is significant, in this connection, that Mulvaney never makes it beyond
corporal, even those heights proving too dizzy for more than a
few weeks or months at a time. Clearly Kipling prefers to keep
him a perpetual private, just as he wanted Indians to remain
Indians—and children, one suspects, children. As such they can
accept discipline and direction from above instead of having to
impose it on themselves. So apparently pointless and unfulfilling
can the disciplined life demanded of Kipling's private soldiers
seem in a story like "Black Jack," however, that the need for
compensations is far more pressing than for most of us. And so

far removed are those compensations—companionship above all, of course, but alcohol and a little forgetfulness when even that fails—from the solid sense of achievement experienced by the world's bridge-builders, that it takes a Mulvaney, with all his capacity for choosing to laugh rather than weep at himself, to step back from the abyss.

Native Indian Stories

In turning to Kipling's native Indian stories, I find it significant that the category includes not only examples of what I judge to be his finest writing about India, but some of the earliest stories he chose to preserve in subsequent collections—stories written before the family's social success in Simla, and before the chance to write a regular column for a known audience became a major factor in deciding his choice of topic.

Earliest of all is "The Gate of the Hundred Sorrows" (1884), a dramatic monologue doubtless owing something to Browning, in which a regular customer hauntingly evokes the atmosphere of an opium den whose habitués do not even notice the abyss into which they are falling. Also told in the first person, and even more esoteric in atmosphere, "In the House of Suddhoo" (1886) seems at first reading to be merely a sensational description of magic and clairvoyance, with a grim twist at the end. As Elliott L. Gilbert has pointed out,[6] however, the callow confidence of the young English narrator at the outset, that he can speedily expose the performance for the fake it undoubtedly is, becomes grimly ironic. He discovers not only that he is powerless to alter the course of events for the better, but that he has become an unwitting accomplice, aggravating rather than resolving the situation. Perhaps the story really belongs in the Anglo-Indian category, as an example of how the young Kipling, uncorrupted by his elders, had a clearer if largely unconscious sense of the Anglo-Indian's true predicament in India.

Much the same is true of "The Strange Ride of Morrowbie Jukes" (1885), where the protagonist is again an Englishman alone among Indians. On a headlong gallop in the late, delirious stages of a fever, Jukes falls, together with his pony, into a steep-sided craterlike depression in the sand on the banks of a river. He wakes in the morning to find it ringed by caves inhabited by Indians who have recovered from seeming death during their burial ceremonies, and accordingly been exiled to this living death. The walls of the crater crumble, he discovers, whenever one tries to climb them, and escape via the river is prevented by quicksands, reinforced during the day by a man in a boat with a gun. Jukes hears his horse being killed by the ravenous inmates, is ostensibly befriended but actually brought step by step down to his own level by a Brahmin he once knew, learns how to catch and cook crows, discovers that the only other Englishman to blunder into this trap was murdered for the secret of the way through the quicksands he had almost finished working out, and nearly dies himself for similar reasons. Only his "inartistic and improbable escape" at the end, argues Angus Wilson, prevents this (written when Kipling was only nineteen) "from being among the first dozen of all Kipling's stories."[7] (Does waking up after a nightmare lessen its impact, or deepen it by juxtaposing normalcy?) As a vision of the Englishman's situation, trapped in a subcontinent with several hundred million envious Indians (and, of course, of a more generalized nightmare sense of living death), the story is little short of Kafkaesque.

Much the same parabolic quality can be seen in the well-known "The Man Who Would Be King" (1888), a story which defies classification under my headings, since the two white adventurers who are its protagonists are the scum of Anglo-Indian society, while the tribes they set out to "civilize" may, it is speculated, be descended from Alexander's army. Can Kipling be scurrilously parodying the British acquisition of India? The story has an elaborate frame, a journalist narrator being party to the mad scheme from the start, and hearing of what happened from the one grotesquely crippled survivor to return. His story includes their luck in getting themselves and their precious cargo of guns into a remote region of warring tribes, their success in training first one tribe and then another to fight in a disciplined fashion till they have established their authority over a large area, and their considerable achievement in bringing peace and prosperity where before there had been perpetual petty warfare. The parallel with the East India Company cannot be unintended, even though, since their ultimate aim is mere plunder, they cannot be allowed to achieve it. All goes well until one of them breaks their self-imposed embargo on women and liquor. For, in choosing a wife for himself, the self-styled emperor of this new nation state discredits the divine status he had until then been accorded, and dies an all too mortal death. The whole story is uncannily perceptive of the dilemma of all conquerors who find the exalted status they accord themselves uncomfortable to maintain. It is also refreshingly honest about the underlying motives of most imperialists. One wonders, however, whether many of its original readers were aware of such implications.

When we turn to stories with Indian protagonists, we find first-person narratives predominating, the corollary of this being the use of a kind of dialect. In later stories, such as "One View of the Question" and "A Sahibs' War," this can constitute a kind of mask to enable Kipling to voice opinions which it might not have been seemly or credible for a white man to do. It can also serve, however, to show differences between one speaker and another. Thus the speaker in "Dray Wara Yow Dee" is established as a passionate frontiersman, in contrast to his more drab counterparts from the plains in "At Howli Thana" or "Gemini" by such turns of speech as "Does a man tear out his heart and make fritters thereof over a slow fire for aught other than a woman?" or "for it was in my heart that I should kill Daoud Shah with my bare hands thus—as a man strips a bunch of raisins." But in the main Kipling's attempt to capture the speaking voice of his Indian characters is intended to give a generically Indian flavor to the whole group of such stories. For the "dialect" used is, of course, a translation into English of grammatical peculiarities and idioms in the Urdu or Hindustani in which we are to suppose the stories were originally told. Hence the use of "thee" and "thou" when equals or inferiors are being addressed, but always of "you" for the Sahib listener and recorder of the tales.

There is also a colorfulness and an eloquence, a love of metaphor and of proverb, and a general relishing of language for language's sake which seems to characterize all Kipling's Indian speakers, and which, like Mulvaney's Irishness, is in sharp contrast to the clipped, cliché-ridden speech, full of self-deprecatory understatement, of his Anglo-Indians in general and his subalterns in particular. Dedicated in so many ways to being the quintessential Englishman, Kipling clearly enjoys the excuse to give language a free rein. Nevertheless, in the very language they are permitted to use, there is the same implication we have already noted: that about Indians and Irishmen and private soldiers (as about children) there is a quality of innocence and openness and spontaneity which Kipling responds to and is in many ways sad to have lost, but which will prevent their ever being other than Indians or Irishmen or private soldiers.

Strangely mixed in its quality as a story, "On the City Wall" falls into two almost unrelated halves and juxtaposes seemingly irreconcilable attitudes and tones of voice. The first half is set in a house on the city wall, a kind of voluptuous salon where Lalun holds court, and to which the English narrator has honorary entrée as the friend of Wali Dad, her favorite admirer. He is a young man totally confused by the clash between his English education and his Indian heritage. Consequently he spends all his days singing songs and making love to Lalun. That he and the others who gather at Lalun's, engaged in endless and totally unproductive conversation, should be presented so sympathetically is unique in Kipling's work, and probably due to the spell cast over him by Lalun. Yet, side by side with this atypical glimpse of a different side to Indian life, we have the most often quoted passage by Kipling in praise of the hardworking British administrators whose untiring efforts make such a butterfly existence possible.

Year by year England sends out fresh drafts for the first fighting-line, which is officially called the Indian Civil Service. These die, or kill themselves by overwork, or are worried to death, or broken in health and hope in order that the land may be protected from death and sickness, famine and war, and may eventually become capable of standing alone. It will never stand alone, but the idea is a pretty one, and men are willing to die for it, and yearly the work of pushing and coaxing and scolding and petting the country into good living goes forward. If an advance be made all credit is given to the native, while the Englishmen stand back and wipe their foreheads. If a failure occurs the Englishmen step forward and take the blame. (4:305–306)

Clearly Kipling idealizes an averagely incompetent bureaucracy. Yet he does so totally without irony, despite the fact that in just the previous paragraph a punning song by Wali Dad in praise of Lalun has implied that her beauty could corrupt even the government, and despite the tone set by the story's opening paragraph, which playfully questions the assumption that the British way of doing things is always best. "Lalun is a member of the most ancient profession in the world," says the narrator.

Lilith was her very-great-grandmama, and that was before the days of Eve, as every one knows. In the West, people say rude things about Lalun's profession, and write lectures about it, and distribute the lectures to young persons in order that Morality may be preserved. In the East, where the profession is hereditary, descending from mother to daughter, nobody writes lectures or takes any notice; and that is a distinct proof of the inability of the East to manage its own affairs. (4:302)

Similarly when Wali Dad contemplates the prospect, should he ever decide to work for a living, the result is surely Forster's model for his famous "Bridge Party" in *A Passage to India*.

"I might wear an English coat and trouser. I might be a leading Muhammadan pleader. I might be received even at the Commissioner's tennis-parties, where the English stand on one side and the natives on the other, in order to promote social intercourse throughout the Empire." (4:321)

From Lalun's window the view includes a huge old fort, where a famous, now aged rebel is imprisoned, ready to provide the link with the second half of the story. This is largely taken up with a communal riot between Hindus and Moslems on a Mohamme-dan holy day. The troops from the fort come to the aid of the police, and all Kipling's latent insensitivity, his perpetual "Public-Schoolboyhood" surfaces. "I am sorry to say," writes the narrator smugly,

that they were all pleased, unholily pleased, at the chance of what they called "a little fun." The senior officers, to be sure, grumbled at having been kept out of bed, and the English troops pretended to be sulky, but there was joy in the hearts of all the subalterns, and whispers ran up and down the line.... "D'you think the beggars will really stand up to us?" "'Hope I shall meet my moneylender there. I owe him more than I can afford." "Oh, they won't let us even unsheath swords." "Hurrah! Up goes the fourth rocket. Fall in, there!" (4:330–31)

After watching the riot for some time, the narrator returns to Lalun's, just in time to help pull an old man through the window whom "the Hindus have been hunting ... with clubs," and escort him across town to a waiting carriage, at Lalun's winsome behest. Only when the news breaks of the old rebel's escape does he realize how he has been used, Wali Dad (how typical of an Indian!) having failed to turn up on time. Fortunately there are no serious consequences. The old rebel finds the young men would rather join a native regiment than follow him to certain death, and turns himself in.

The story is something of a compendium of Kipling's varied and contradictory attitudes toward British and Indians alike in an India under British rule. This pervasive ambivalence is most intriguingly brought out in the narrator's own feelings toward Lalun—an embodiment of India herself, surely. He must therefore remain an admiring onlooker only, since she belongs to Wali Dad, and to the other conspirators who use her to further their cause. Nevertheless, he finds himself susceptible enough to her charms to be used in his turn—to be corrupted by her, as the song claimed the government would be. Both the narrator and Wali Dad have in some sense been seduced by the other side. Yet what this potentially subtle story lacks is a single, ironically ambivalent tone throughout. What we have, rather, is an overall naïve charm as real but incompatible loyalties and likings are set down cheek by jowl with artless honesty. By no means Kipling's most remarkable Indian story, "On the City Wall" may well be the most revealing of Kipling himself.

A story which does have a claim to be his most remarkable piece of short fiction about Indians is the deeply moving and often praised "Without Benefit of Clergy," which tells of the marriage, however unblessed by clergy, of an Indian girl and an Anglo-Indian administrator. Written after Kipling's return to England, it is perhaps too bold to have first appeared in the *Pioneer*. Yet he had published several stories in India which treated of sexual relations between the races, the most striking being "Beyond the Pale." This opens with a platitude from the narrator which, along with the title, is clearly intended to elicit nods of sage approval: "A man should, whatever happens, keep to his own caste, race and breed" (1:189). Yet no reader, however much in agreement with such sentiments, can recall those words in the same frame of mind, once having read the story. Not when the horrifying fate of the fifteen-year-old Hindu widow, her relatives having discovered that she is being visited secretly by an Englishman, is contrasted with the casual if quite genuine pleasure the visitor takes in this unspoiled child of nature. The truth of the axiom has been more than amply demonstrated (and, with an added irony, demonstrated as a result of *Indian* intolerance). Yet it can no longer be subscribed to with the same complacency.

But to return to "Without Benefit of Clergy,"[8] the story tells ot an Englishman's impulsively buying a young Indian girl from her greedy mother, of their growing love for one another, of how the birth of a son still further enriches their love as his death still further deepens it, and of the eventual death of the girl. It has been read as a cautionary tale exemplifying the same sad truth that a man should keep to his own caste, race, and breed;[9] if it had not been cholera it would have been slower but no less fatal social pressures which put an end to their love. But the love described is of the kind which takes its whole quality from the very fact of its being enjoyed for each moment's sake, irrespective of what the future brings. It is in fact intensified not only by the strangeness, the newness of each of the lovers for the other, and by the need to keep their life together a precarious secret, but also by the recurring threats to its permanence. Whether ended by cholera or social pressures or sheer old age, it will still have been worth the having, and whatever is lost as a result of it will have been well lost.

What neither of the lovers loses is his or her essential Englishness or Indianness, each rather adding something to it. John Holden still puts in an appearance at the club after returning from a temporary posting elsewhere, even though longing to see his wife and the child which has probably been born to him in the interim. Likewise, after a reunion almost too fraught with joy to be borne, he returns to the club to pull himself together, the blood of the goats he was required to sacrifice still on his boots. His own tribal rituals are still necessary. But they, and the reprimand he receives for not having had his mind on his work during his temporary posting, are viewed with a sense of proportion rare in Kipling, for whom rituals and the work ethic too often seem paramount. Similarly, Ameera continues to perform all the appropriate rituals for averting harm to the child's and their happiness. After the child's death, moreover, both parents are more secretive than ever about their love, as if to propitiate or avoid attracting the attention of whatever might begrudge them their joy in one another. When Holden offers to send her to the hills in the hot weather, however, she scorns this white woman's precaution against misfortune, if it means leaving her man behind. Life itself is so provisional a commodity in India that today's happiness is too precious to be traded for some hypothetically more lasting or worthwhile happiness tomorrow. So, when cholera strikes the city, they abandon the superstitious concealment of their love, "calling each other by every pet name that could move the wrath of the gods." At last Ameera has recognized that, aside from that which there is no defense against, their happiness is threatened by and needs protection from no one but themselves. So much so that her dying words are, "I bear witness—I bear witness—that there is no god but—thee, beloved" (4:134).

Once again the best and most interesting stories are those involving both Indians and Anglo-Indians. The Anglo-Indians, moreover, are all shown, in the stories we have considered, as having more to learn from the Indians than vice versa (as in "Without Benefit of Clergy"), or as being much more circumscribed in their power to control the situations in which they find themselves than Sahibs were supposed to be.

There are, of course, very many Indian stories we have not considered. Kipling wrote nearly 120 of them—numerically almost half his life's output. There is, for instance, a group including "Only a Subaltern," "A Conference of the Powers," "The Brushwood Boy," and "The Tomb of His Ancestors," in which Kipling idealizes the young subalterns of his Indian army. These embodiments of the pure elixir of youth, willingly submitting and lending their strength to the tired wisdom of age, we shall return to when considering young Roman officers in later stories. Then there is a whole subcategory about children, including "The Story of Muhammad Din" and "Little Tobrah" (rare miniatures about the precarious beauties and all too prevalent horrors of Indian childhood), "Tods' Amendment" (advice to legislators from a diminutive Anglo-Indian who knows more about what the "real Indians" think than they do), and "Drums of the Fore and Aft" (drummer boys to the rescue when the regiment turns tail). As some compensation, we shall now consider what is not only Kipling's finest story about India, but one of the best books about childhood in the language.

Kim

Begun while Kipling was living in Brattleboro, *Kim* was not completed until he had returned to England. More important, it was completed in close collaboration with Lockwood (and to a lesser extent Alice) Kipling. The author would read completed chapters to them, and discuss with them many aspects of life in India about which the scholarly father, who had by then lived there for most of thirty years, knew far more than the son. (His portrait, as the museum curator, appears in the first chapter.) A sense of audience often seems to have been important to Kipling. We have seen how his early Anglo-Indian stories were tailored to a particular readership. And we shall see how the pleasure he took in telling stories to children is reflected in the style of those he wrote for them. So the fact that *Kim* was written in the first place for this select readership of two seasoned but enlightened Anglo-Indians probably had no small influence on the book.

What everyone remembers about *Kim* is the way we are invited to share a child's fascinated wonder at the sheer multiplicity and color and variety of India's teeming millions. The fact that the protagonist is a child frees Kipling from the need to pass inhibiting judgments on what he sees, and makes us realize that he must have had the capacity for such delight all along. The occupants of a third-class railway compartment; professional letter writers and the gimcrack baroque of their English prose style; a handsome hill woman summoning her husbands to carry the Lama's litter; the young prostitute who helps disguise Kim; quiet Jain priests wishing the Buddhist Lama well in his search, in sharp contrast to the mutual suspicions of a Church of England and a Catholic padre; the garrulous old widow exchanging insults with the world from the curtained bullock-cart in which she is traveling; and above all the pageant of Indian life making its way along the Grand Trunk Road: such are some of the vignettes one remembers of even very minor characters.

But the book reveals the strength of Kipling's feelings for Indian India, and the surprising extent to which he sympathized with an Eastern as opposed to a Western philosophy of life, at a much more profound level than that of a response to the picturesque. In the first place, Kim himself "was white—a poor white of the very poorest," orphan of a young Irish color sergeant and an equally Irish mother. Yet, though clearly retaining a degree of inherent, inborn self-assurance in his dealings with Indians, he in fact much prefers to pass for an Indian and live the role he has grown up playing most of his childhood. (Irish, like Mulvaney, and a child to boot, he is free to do and be what Kipling—or at all events that side of Kipling which he may well have regarded as the Celtic half of his makeup—could only enjoy vicariously.) And in the second place, unashamedly picaresque in structure, the book combines the disparate quests of its improbably yoked Don Quixote and Sancho Panza in a manner which at least allows them to co-exist, if not coalesce.

For when Kim decides to become the Lama's *chela*, joining him in his quest for the River of Healing, and in the meantime piloting him through the treacherous shallows of everyday duplicity in India, the boy remembers words of his father about a red bull on a green field which was the god of those who would one day make a man of him. So he provides himself with his own subsidiary quest. And when Kim finds something at least of what he seeks, in the form of his father's old regiment and its flag, the joint quest is interrupted while Kim is sent to school. Not only must the Lama pursue his pilgrimage to all the holy places of Buddhism alone, without much hope that he will find his river until rejoined by his heaven-sent *chela*, but he actually pays for Kim's education. Finally, in the six months grace Kim is allowed between leaving school and taking up his duties in the secret service, for which he has been singled out and trained on the side during the school holidays, he rejoins the Lama. All too easily, however, the latter is persuaded to direct his search northward toward his native hills, so that Kim can assist another agent in keeping an eye on the spying activities of a Russian and a Frenchman. Kim earns great credit for his part in the adventure. But the Lama, in a bruising encounter with the two Europeans, is almost provoked to answer violence with violence. With curiously inverse symbolism, he must return to the plains to resume his search for the highest in more propitious surroundings.

From such a summary it would appear that Kim is more of a hindrance than a help to the Lama in his quest, and that their aims in life are totally and indeed ludicrously incompatible.

"Then all Doing is evil?" Kim replied, lying out under a big tree at the fork of the Doon road, watching the little ants run over his hand.

"To abstain from action is well—except to acquire merit."

"At the Gates of Learning we were taught that to abstain from action was unbefitting a Sahib. And I am a Sahib." (19:347)

Kim, moreover, is incorrigibly and insatiably a child of this world, from whose illusions the Lama would free him.

Often the lama made the living pictures the matter of his text, bidding Kim—*too ready*—note how the flesh takes a thousand thousand shapes, desirable or detestable as men reckon, but in truth of no account either way.... (19:347, italics added)

Greatest irony of all, the Lama has had his monastery pay for Kim to acquire the white man's wisdom, which will equip him not as the old man is allowed to believe to be a scribe, but to become a spy and play his part in the Great Game. Perhaps the greatest incompatibility of all, however, is that Kim's inner quest is clearly a Western one for a sense of identity, for selfhood, and therefore symbolized by a road which leads somewhere. The Lama's, on the other hand, is for loss of self, annihilation of identity—for escape from a wheel or circle that leads nowhere. Just how incompatible these attitudes are is well illustrated by Kim's interior monologue.

"Well is the Game called great! I was four days a scullion at Quetta, waiting on the wife of the man whose book I stole. And that was part of the Great Game! From the South—God knows how far—came up the Mahratta, playing the Great Game in fear of his life. Now I shall go far and far into the North playing the Great Game. Truly, it runs like a shuttle throughout all Hind. And my share and my joy"—he smiled to the darkness—"I owe to the lama here. Also to Mahbub Ali—also to Creighton Sahib, but chiefly to the Holy One. He is right—a great and a wonderful world—and I am Kim—Kim—Kim—alone—one person—in the middle of it all." (19:368)

Whatever the Lama meant to teach him, it was not, surely, that the world is great and wonderful in quite this kind of way.

A much more successful reconciliation of the values of East and West might seem to have been achieved in "The Miracle of the Puran Bhagat," from *The Second Jungle Book*, written just before Kipling began work on *Kim*. In it Sir Puran Bhagat, K.C.I.E., reforming prime minister of a native Indian state and toast of the smart set in London, takes to the road with his begging bowl, to become a holy man in his declining years. Having settled on a small shrine in the hills as his final place of meditation, where he is fed and revered by the local villagers and waited on by the local monkeys, he realizes, one night of heavy rain, that a landslide is imminent which will obliterate both shrine and village. Here perhaps is the perfect, unsolicited release he seeks from endless cycles of existence. Yet, with scarcely a moment's hesitation, he becomes once more the man of action, warning the villagers and organizing their evacuation. Happily his dearest wish is not denied, and he dies from his exertions once they are all safe.

Somewhat similarly in *Kim*, when the Lama has returned to the plains and Kim is in a prolonged sleep, recovering from the journey, the old man has a vision of his desired release—seems, indeed, to have attained it.

"Yea, my Soul went free, and, wheeling like an eagle, saw indeed that there was no Teshoo Lama nor any other soul. As a drop draws to water, so my soul drew near to the Great Soul which is beyond all things. At that point, exalted in contemplation, I saw all Hind, from Ceylon in the sea to the Hills, and my own Painted Rocks at Suchzen; I saw every camp and village, to the least, where we have ever rested. I saw them at one time and in one place; for they were within the Soul. By this I knew the Soul had passed beyond the illusion of Time and Space and of Things. By this I knew that I was free." (19:471–72)

But this is not yet to be.

"Then a voice cried: 'What shall come to the boy if thou art dead?' and I was shaken back and forth in myself with pity for thee; and I said: 'I will return to my *chela*, lest he miss the Way.' Upon this my Soul, which is the soul of Teshoo Lama, withdrew itself from the Great Soul with strivings and yearnings and retchings and agonies not to be told. As the egg from the fish, as the fish from the water, as the water from the cloud, as the cloud from the thick air, so put forth, so leaped out, so drew away, so fumed up the soul of Teshoo Lama from the Great Soul." (19:472)

And as with Puran Bhagat, his concern for others and his last-minute conversion to a Western code of concerned involvement and of action are rewarded.

"Then a voice cried: 'The River! Take heed to the River!' and I looked down upon all the world, which was as I had seen it before—one in time, one in place—and I saw plainly the River of the Arrow at my feet." (19:472–73)

Thus both stories seem to end with a marriage of East and West, action and comtemplation, worldliness and otherworldliness. But in the case of *Kim* we are still left acutely aware, the Lama having at such cost wrenched his soul "back from the Threshold of Freedom" to show his *chela* the Way, that Kim's self-discovery has taken the form of an apprenticeship for the Great Game, in which the Lama has played a quite unwitting part. And we are all too uneasily conscious that this Great Game, Kim's enthusiastic participation in it, and indeed his whole boyish delight at life's variety and adventure, are totally at odds with the deliverance the Lama seeks to win for him. The book may well still seem an irredeemable mishmash of John Buchan and the Eightfold Path.

Yet it is perhaps in just some such irreconcilable juxtaposition that the book's quality consists. Kim does not judge, Kipling does not judge, we are not asked to judge, the rightness or wrongness of the Lama's way, of Creighton Sahib's Great Game, or of Mahbub Ali's fierce code of honor and relish in the delights of the flesh. The whole atmosphere of the book is inimical to the making of judgments. Even Kipling's most persistent prejudices vanish, for Huree Babu, one of Creighton's star agents and Kim's skillful ally in thwarting the spies in the mountains, is a fat, often-frightened, university-educated Bengali, akin to those ridiculed in "The Head of the District." The very fact that a Tibetan Buddhist should play so central a role indicates, perhaps, that Kipling wants to call a truce between Moslem and Hindu, between Mahbub and Huree. The only characters to be "judged" and to come out of the book badly are the Russian who provokes the Lama to anger in the hills and the Anglican padre of the Mavericks (the latter cutting a very poor figure alongside his far from perfect Catholic counterpart). Both are white; both are intolerant and uncomprehending in their attitude to India's baffling variousness. Both are everything the book is not.

And what that is, in the first instance, is a world of romance—a world full of horse thieves and prostitutes and bribery and murder, yet as innocent of real evil as Kim himself. For, as untouched by it all as Pippa, and as deserving of our trust through the innate rightness of his choices as Huck, Kim plays a role quite other than theirs. His not to shed a ray of light in a world of darkness or to act as a touchstone whereby the cruelty and hypocrisy around him can be seen for what they are. His, rather, to celebrate the world's richness and variety as only the naïve eye of a child can. This, Kipling's last and most successful backward look at India, is also a supremely successful recapturing of the world of childhood, as viewed nostalgically by the adult.

Indeed, for all the knowingness of the one and the wisdom of the other, Kim and his Lama are equally naïve and equally sanguine in their outlook. Yet this does not result in a simplistic portrayal of things. For not only are the wordly child's-eye view of one and the otherwordly saint's-eye view of the other juxtaposed, seemingly irreconcilably. Each to some extent incorporates the other. The inner drama of the Lama is that his quest for the River of Life reawakens his attachment and responsiveness to, even his love for, this world of shadows. He remembers a singing game of a woman with her baby and repeats it to a village child. He all but strikes a man in anger. He bids farewell once more to his beloved hills as "shadows blessed above all other shadows." But above even his hills he loves his young *chela*. And *Kim*? He, of course, has no real understanding of what the Lama

means by the Way, and insofar as he does understand it he
recognizes it as radically at odds with just about everything he
finds most fascinating. Yet he loves him. To Mahbub's tolerant
puzzlement, of all those Kim meets in the life of intrigue and
adventure he is entering on, it is the Lama who takes precedence.
Right at the heart of a book which emphasizes abundance and
variety, caught in the amber of an old man and a boy's caring
deeply for each other, lies the ultimate, irreconcilable, yet continuing and enriching dichotomy of matter and spirit. The world *is* a
mishmash of Buchan and Buddha.

In arguing for so pervasive a nonjudgmental quality to the
book, I am happy to disagree with Edmund Wilson, who wanted
Kim to judge between the values of India and those of British
imperialism, choosing the former and rejecting the latter.[10] Wilson asks the impossible of Kipling, of course, in the form not only
of a hero who rejects the British raj, but of one who undergoes
prolonged self-doubt and self-examination. But it is far from
clear that the book would have been a better one than it is, even if
Kipling had been capable of writing to Wilson's prescription. I
am less happy about seeming to quarrel with Mark Kinkead-
Weekes's sensitive study of Kipling's novels,[11] in which he argues
that Kipling does require us to pass judgment on the Lama's
values on the one hand and those of the Russians and the English
alike on the other. He sees the two crucial turning points, at
which such an act of judgment is called for, as being the Lama's
encounter with the two Christian chaplains, when Kim first finds
his father's regiment, and the blow the Russian agent (and the
whole world of action he stands for) strikes at the Lama. With his
veiw of the first of these I would almost wholly concur. The
memory of the Lama's quiet dignity and wisdom, and of the
ignorant contempt with which he is judged by these two men of
God (and by one in particular), casts a shadow over the whole of
Kim's subsequent education, paid for by the Lama for its own
sake, but exploited by a variety of white men for a variety of
ulterior ends. Nevertheless, equally crucial as the second of these
crises may be, I cannot agree that, after it, "We should need very
strong evidence ... to support the idea that Kim could return to

the Game against the whole current of the book's disabling criticism." [12] On the contrary, nothing in the book suggests that Kim in any way equates the Russian's role in the Great Game with his own or Creighton's or Mahbub Ali's. To argue otherwise is to want to rewrite the book as radically as Edmund Wilson does.

Kim's thoughts on the precious documents stolen from the Russian, for example—"If someone duly authorized would only take delivery of them the Great Game might play itself for all he *then* cared" (19:444, italics added)—are no reliable guide as to what he will do for the rest of his days. At that moment he is just too weighed down by them as physical objects, as well as by the responsibility of caring for a suddenly frail Lama. Indeed, having handed them over to Huree Babu, and having heard his side of the story, Kim's reaction is quite different.

"He robbed them," thought Kim, forgetting his own share in the game. "He tricked them. He lied to them like a Bengali. They gave him a *chit* (a testimonial). He makes them a mock at the risk of his life—*I* never would have gone down to them after the pistol-shots—and then he says he is a fearful man.... And he *is* a fearful man. I must get into the world again." (19:461)

The world he is so anxious to rejoin, moreover, though his legs still bend "like bad pipe-stems," is essentially Kim's world.

Roads were meant to be walked upon, houses to be lived in, cattle to be driven, fields to be tilled, and men and women to be talked to. They were all real and true—solidly planted upon the feet—perfectly comprehensible—clay of his clay, neither more nor less. (19:462–63)

Kinkead-Weekes feels bound to admit of the author that the extraordinary sympathy he achieves in this book with a character "almost at the furthest possible remove from Kipling himself.... enabling him to see, think and feel *beyond* himself," is unique to *Kim* and "never happened again." [13] I should prefer to say, with Edmund Wilson, that "we are to meet this Lama again in strange and unexpected forms still haunting that practical world which Kipling, like Kim, has chosen."[14] But the important point to be made is that what is true of Kim's creator is equally true of Kim himself. Both belong too firmly to a world of action and of games, great and small, to abandon it, however illuminated it has momentarily been, and may continue to be from time to time, by a more rarefied spiritual reality—yet not, for all its depth of insight, a more real or valid reality. For the Lama, when he returns from union with the Great Soul for love of his *chela*, is enabled then and then only to discover his River—a river that has been there, at his feet, waiting to be discovered all his life. The world of shadows, too, has its own validity, and is part of the totality which, momentarily and precariously, *Kim* presents us with, whole. We do not want to know what Kim did next. We are content with a moment of equilibrium.

Conclusion

In some ways Kipling's whole output of stories about India can be viewed as a search for equilibrium, whether between East and West, action and contemplation, or youth and age. So many of them turn out, ultimately, to be about a balance between the "civilization" and discipline the British try to impose on India, or his commanding officer on Mulvaney, and the variety, the richness, the vitality, even the intractable wisdom of the raw material these artists of law and order seek to imbue with their sense of form. And any such balance is a model, of course, of what Kipling the artist was striving to achieve in his writing. Occasionally the control is insufficient and chaos threatens to take over—as in "The Incarnation of Krishna Mulvaney," perhaps, and some of the later Pyecroft stories. More often the control is too obvious, as in one or two of the neater *Plain Tales from the Hills* or "A Walking Delegate" and "The Mother Hive." Relatively seldom, however, does one find such imbalance in the Indian stories. Perhaps this is because they were written at a time when Kipling felt the exhilaration of walking a tightrope more or less success-fully between a discipline he respected and a chaos he both feared and was attracted by. In later years he was more likely to find himself sitting well to one side of the fence and deploring what he saw on the other. Certainly he never again gave expression to the duality of life so perfectly as he did in *Kim*.

> Something I owe to the soil that grew—
>   More to the life that fed—
> But most to Allah Who gave me two
>   Separate sides to my head.
>
> I would go without shirts or shoes,
>   Friends, tobacco or bread
> Sooner than for an instant lose
>   Either side of my head. (19:214)

Chapter Three
Stories for Children

Like most categories, that of children's literature has a firm core and fuzzy edges. In Kipling's case, moreover, the frontier regions of his adult fiction can be equally disputable territory. It is often impossible to say with certainty for which category of readers he is writing. This indicates, on the one hand, that he had too much respect for children to talk down to them or oversimplify things on their behalf. And on the other it probably betrays his hankering after a childhood he lost almost before it began. Having scarcely been allowed to be a child, Kipling in some ways never really became an adult.

The most obvious and successful example of such facing-both-ways writing is *Kim*, already discussed as a book for adults. As Kipling's only successful novel, moreover, *Kim* is representative of his writing for children in being a unified whole. For this seems to be a characteristic of most of what he wrote for children and very little of what he wrote for adults. Even the collections of stories for children, like the *Just So Stories* and *The Jungle Books*, are held together by a shared style or subject matter. In most cases, in fact, his books for children have a much clearer and frequently more didactic unifying theme than those for adults. This is clumsily obvious in *Captains Courageous*, but is also borne out by the insistent emphasis on the "Law" in the Mowgli stories, and by the recurring, almost fatalistic motif of "What else could I/he/she/they have done?" running through *Rewards and Fairies*. With few exceptions, however, such didacticism offers anything but a simplistically reductive view of the world. As a rule, Kipling pays his young readers the compliment of presenting, under what may seem a deceptively simple surface, a truly complex and often equivocal view of things. Indeed, writing of *Rewards and Fairies*, Kipling combines an admission that the book is as much for adults as for children with a description of the kinds of complexity he came increasingly to strive for in his writing.

Yet, since the tales had to be read by children, before people realized that they were meant for grown-ups, and since they had to be a sort of balance to, as well as a seal upon, some aspects of my imperialistic output in the past, I worked the material in three or four overlaid tints and textures, which might or might not reveal themselves according to the shifting light of sex, youth and experience. It was like working lacquer and mother o' pearl, a natural combination, into the same scheme as niello and grisaille, and trying not to let the joints show. (36:182–83)

Such stratification is to be found, in a simplified form, even in the *Just So Stories*. Children realize, of course, that the explanation of "How the Rhinoceros Got his Skin" is not to be taken entirely seriously. But in a post-Darwin world, the joke for the adult in the book's seven or eight mock myths of natural history has at least an extra layer. And in "The Crab that Played," Kipling is not content merely to account for the crab's shell and pincers. He begins, seeming to draw on authentically mythic levels of imagination, with a creation story where everything goes according to plan except for one oversight.[1] But he ends, having cut an enormous king crab down to size who was making the sea flood the land twice a day, by substituting a protoscientific explanation and transferring the responsibility for tugging the sea around in tides to the fisherman in the moon. Some of the later stories, such as "The Cat that Walked by Himself" and "The Butterfly that Stamped," probably appeal more to the adult reading aloud than to the child listening. But the success of the collection as a whole depends very much on its simultaneous appeal to both reader and listener. Kipling knew that no child can really enjoy being read to by someone who is not also enjoying himself, any more than an adult can enjoy reading to a child who is bored.

The supreme example of this simultaneous appeal to adult and child is without doubt "The Elephant's Child." The climax of the story for the child is presumably the Elephant's Child's use of his new trunk to spank "all his dear families for a long time till they were very warm and greatly astonished," and sufficiently convinced, moreover, of the usefulness of this new appendage to depart "one by one in a hurry to the banks of the great grey-green, greasy Limpopo River, all set about with fever trees, to borrow new noses from the Crocodile" (20:85). But it is the author's unashamed enjoyment of language which, communicating itself to the adult as performer as much as to the child as listener, is the story's crowning glory. Best loved are such gleefully anticipated and alliteratively grandiose formulae as "great grey-green, greasy..." and "scalesome flailsome tail." But scarcely less memorable are the varied speech patterns of the characters, from the Elephant's Child's "'Scuse me, but have you seen such a thing as a Crocodile in these promiscuous parts?" to the Bi-Coloured-Python-Rock-Snake's "Rash and inexperienced traveller, we will now seriously devote ourselves to a little high tension, because if we do not, it is my impression that..." (20:75).

I find it difficult to credit that, as a serious young adult, I once disliked this story intensely. I found the exploitation of such supposedly childish solecisms as "'satiable curtiosity" or "promiscuous parts," and such knowing authorial comments as "when there was nothing left of the Equinoxes, because the Precession had preceded according to precedent" or "and he wept crocodile tears to show it was quite true," quite intolerable. Directed with so obvious a wink over the child's shoulder at the adult reading, they seemed insufferably condescending. (As if most of the adults would have had any clearer idea what a precession of the equinoxes was than the children they were reading to!) Having since read the story with equal success to five-year-olds, twelve-year-olds, twenty-year-olds, and seventy- or eighty-year-olds, I can only think that I was suffering from too acute a case of our own century's mistrust of rhetoric to enjoy enjoying language for its own sake. Grant only that the story is written to be performed rather than merely read, and the shared pleasure of author, reader, and listener subsumes any such exclusiveness.

The *Just So Stories* are for children younger than the presumed readership of anything else Kipling wrote, but his earliest works for children were the two *Jungle Books,*[2] written before he had any of his own old enough to be read to. And therein lies a curious difference. The *Just So Stories* are clearly the literary versions of stories composed in an oral tradition. Moreover, though Josephine was dead before most of them were written down, one senses her presence throughout. All but three are directly addressed to "My best beloved," and she is clearly a participant in the three stories about Taffy, that precocious only child of her neolithic daddy, Tegumai. Similarly, *Puck of Pook's Hill* and *Rewards and Fairies* were written for Elsie and John Kipling, who, as Una and Dan, provide a narrative frame of the kind often favored by Kipling in his later, more complex fiction. This not only anchors each story, no matter how historically remote or exotic, to the here and now, but introduces complexities as to how much the listeners within the story, let alone those outside it, can understand of what is going on.

But in the *Jungle Books* there are narrative frames to very few of the stories, and only a minimum of explanatory intrusions by the author. With two exceptions, these stories are less elaborately, less fussily told than most of Kipling's later ones. This leaves them free to achieve a magical kind of realism which, in a story like "The White Seal," is contemporary with or earlier than the work of such North American pioneers in realistic animal fiction as Ernest Thompson Seton, Charles Roberts, and Jack London. Even the Mowgli stories, unashamedly anthropomorphic in so many ways, present a quite unsentimental picture of the realities of nature.

Yet the exploits of Rikki Tikki Tavi and the White Seal also have an almost folk- or fairy-tale quality to them. And the Mowgli story as a whole, of course, captures that ultimate juvenile male fantasy, beyond those even of *Robinson Crusoe* and *Coral Island,* of growing up totally in the wild—and almost wholly free from feminine interference. Not content with realism and fantasy or romance, however, Kipling adds a strongly (though never smotheringly) didactic layer. It was the didacticism, obviously, which so attracted Baden Powell and led to his adopting the Mowgli stories as the underlying mythology of the

Wolf Cubs. And very convincingly does Kipling present the overriding need of his jungle world for a Law—a Law which is at one and the same time biological and social, as inescapable as the former, as moral as the latter, till the distinctions blur. The ecological good sense of not killing more than one needs to eat, for instance, becomes part of the Edenic harmony which exists between Mowgli and his fellow jungle creatures.

Curiously, however, very few specific laws are mentioned which might apply to human Wolf Cubs. ("Wash daily from nose-tip to tail-tip" is about the only one that springs to mind.) What dominates all the stories, on the other hand, is the general message of the concluding and climactic couplet to Kipling's poetic rendering of the Law.

> Now these are the Laws of the Jungle, and many
> and mighty are they;
> But the head and the hoof of the Law and the haunch
> and the hump is—Obey!   (7:105)

And this is the message Kipling clearly most wanted to convey.

Indeed, Noel Annan has argued persuasively that Kipling's chief contribution to what might seem an unlikely field of endeavor for him, the history of ideas, is to have given fictional flesh and blood to theories of Durkheim and other like-minded sociologists.[3] These state that the most important characteristic of law is that it should exist and for the most part be obeyed, irrespective of how well it matches up to some supposed absolute. Law is in fact necessary quite apart from and more importantly than for its moral insights. And nowhere does Kipling maintain such a point of view more insistently than here, in his first work for children. The Banderlog (monkeys) are depicted as both despicable and ineffective, not through disregarding any particular law, but through lack of respect for all law. The wolf pack itself disintegrates at one point into mere anarchy, again not through disregarding any particular law or moral principle, but through having turned its back on the whole concept of law. And eventually they discover, who had once been proud to call themselves the Free People, in what their freedom had consisted. "Lead us again, O Akela. Lead us again, O Man-cub, for we be sick of this lawlessness, and we would be Free People once more" (7:134).

Insofar as any judgment is called for on such a message, today's youth can take little harm and much good from the idea that true freedom lies in a willing submission to something other than self. Such overt didacticism far from exhausts these stories, however. And above all, beyond the message, beyond the memorable characterization of Mowgli's mentors, Baloo, Bagheera, and Kaa, beyond the admirably clear prose style, with just enough of the archaic to suggest an older, saner world than man's, lies the myth. For Mowgli, like Rousseau's noble savage, like Edgar Rice Burroughs's Tarzan, like William Golding's neanderthals, is a post-Enlightenment Adam.[4] From the first he is idyllically at one with all around him.

The boy could climb almost as well as he could swim, and swim almost as well as he could run; so Baloo, the Teacher of the Law, taught him the Wood and Water Laws: how to tell a rotten branch from a sound one; how to speak politely to the wild bees when he came upon a hive of them fifty feet above ground; what to say to Mang, the Bat, when he disturbed him in the branches at midday; and how to warn the water-snakes in the pools before he splashed down among them. (7:35–36)

Yet from the time when the wolves reject him, in "Mowgli's Brothers," and he *names* them "*sag* [dogs], as a man should" (7:28), he clearly enjoys Adam's authority over the animals as well as his uncorrupted kinship with them. Bagheera is astonished, in "Letting in the Jungle," that even Hathi the elephant, "Master of the Jungle," obeys the summons of "Mowgli, the Frog." Clearly, also, he antedates Cain, refusing to allow the shedding of human blood. Indeed, within the terms of the jungle's own Eden myth, as recounted by Hathi in "How Fear Came," he antedates the Fall, since he can outstare Shere Khan even on the one night of the year when no other man can. And in the final story, "Spring Running," he appears to his foster-mother as a "Godling of the Woods ... , strong, tall, and beautiful, his long black hair sweeping over his shoulders, the knife swinging at his neck, and his head crowned with a wreath of white jasmine" (7:280).

Yet there are differences. The Eden Kipling describes is very much a post-Darwin one. Mowgli is an unashamed meat-eater, as are all his close companions. The much earlier and more traditionally Edenic state of affairs described by Hathi, after the jungle's creation, when "there was no drought, and leaves and flowers and fruit grew on the same tree, and we ate nothing at all except leaves and flowers and grass and fruit and bark" (7:90), is rejected scornfully not only by Bagheera the panther, but seemingly by Kipling, who makes Hathi portray the coming of death and dearth as largely the result of undisciplined boredom, which could only be cured by that stern taskmaster and disciplinarian Fear.

When contrasted with the jungle, man as represented by the villagers is clearly fallen. Mowgli's protracted destruction of the village has almost the quality of a ritual cleansing by nature.

I have seen and smelled the blood of the woman that gave me food—the woman whom they would have killed but for me. Only the smell of the new grass on their door-steps can take away that smell. (7:174–75)

Moreover, man's surrogates within the jungle, the Banderlog, are even more scornfully rejected by Mowgli and the other animals. Yet the jungle itself is far from without fault. Shere Khan ignores its Law as he pleases, and successfully tempts many of the wolves into doing the same. Clearly what we are presented with, though strongly Edenic by contrast with the villagers, is realistically or postlapsarianly so. Nor in Kipling's version of the story does Adam, or Mowgli, "fall" from Paradise. Twice he is exiled, once by the wolves and once of his own volition. But in neither case has he broken the Law, and in neither case is he barred from all re-entry. His final departure, being in fact his exile from childhood, is therefore much closer in spirit to "Ode on Intimations of Immortality" than to "Paradise Lost." The loss is one which could not have been avoided, and for which there may be adequate if not abundant compensations.

Such nostalgia, for the childhood of the species as well as of the individual, we have encountered already in Kipling's fondness whether for the uneducated tribesman or for Mulvaney the Irishman. When the former begins to acquire Western ways and education, or when the latter acquires so much as a corporal's stripes, their Edenic incorruptibility is threatened by the responsibilities which crowd in on them.

For the most part, of course, the reader is not consciously aware of such melancholy considerations. Child and adult alike shiver at the eerie spell cast by Kaa over the monkey people, even Baloo and Bagheera having to be rescued from falling under it by Mowgli's touch, in "Kaa's Hunting." Child and adult alike glow with pride at Mowgli's clever generalship in "Tiger, Tiger," and share Bagheera's perturbed awe at his sustained fixity of purpose in "Letting in the Jungle." Adult and (with a little help, perhaps) child alike admire Bagheera's skill and sympathize with his incredulity as he unravels the mysteries of that jungle version of *The Pardoner's Tale,* "The King's Ankus." And in equal measure, if not with equal awareness of earlier literary models, adult and child respond to the uncannily heroic quality Kipling bestows on a snarling squabble between wolves and dogs in "Red Dog."[5]

Coupled with the epic sadness of Akela's death at the end of "Red Dog," however, we have Mowgli's renewed sadness at his inevitable and impending return to the world of men in the next story, "Spring Running." And in this, the last and most melancholy of the stories, we are reminded of the sadness that was a part of Mowgli's anger and scorn in the first story of the collection, when the wolves exiled him from the jungle. We remember, too, his anger with the villagers in "Letting in the Jungle," and suspect, perhaps, that it owed something to his reluctance to acknowledge that these are the creatures with whom he must share his manhood. Truly these stories can evoke a richness and a complexity of response unequaled in almost all earlier books written specifically for children, and unsuspected by those who see in them merely a healthy respect for law and order.

Captains Courageous and *Stalky & Co.*

Kipling's next two children's books, *Captains Courageous* and *Stalky & Co.*, are probably his least interesting. *Captains Courageous* contains a great deal of detailed writing about fishing on the Grand Banks, and illustrates Kipling's increasing preoccupation with the skills of men who are masters of their craft. But the book lacks almost all psychological interest. Harvey, the spoiled son of a millionaire, falls off an ocean liner bound for Europe from New York and is rescued by a Gloucester fishing boat, the *We're Here*. At first he assumes they will make straight for port and the reward his father will pay. And when the skipper laughs at his tales of wealth, he is furious. But he is cured at a single blow of everything in his makeup which could have provided either internal or external drama. For the remainder of the four-month fishing season he works his passage cheerfully, is friends with everyone, and has nothing further to learn than how to be a good sailor. Then, on their return to Gloucester, the self-made millionaire father, who has hitherto left all decisions concerning this son of his to his wife, perceives that someone else has made a man of him and welcomes him aboard as an equal and as a partner. No recriminations, no bitterness; just a clean start, and everything becomes plain sailing.

The book gives us some clue, perhaps, as to why Kipling stayed with the short story so faithfully. Within its confines characters are much less likely to undergo change. And if they do, readers are as a rule ready to accept the fact with only a hint or two as to how and why. Almost all of Kipling's characters, in fact, being as little given to introspection as he himself was, are drawn from the outside. So the best way to read *Captains Courageous* is perhaps as an expanded short story—a kind of parable, where psychology can always be skimped for the sake of the moral. And the moral, in this case, has much less to do with the right way to bring up a boy than with the contrast, as Kinkead-Weekes has pointed out, between the artificial world aboard the liner and the real world aboard the appropriately named *We're Here*.[6] In the former, Harvey can say of the fishing boats "squawking" around them in the fog, "Say, wouldn't it be great if we ran one down" (12:3). (He is, of course, merely tactlessly articulating the values by which both crew and passengers live.) Then, aboard the *We're Here*, which is all but run down herself, he helps rescue a man who has lost his ship, his livelihood, his crew, and (he thinks) his son, to a passing liner.

Stalky & Co. is probably read today, and may in fact always have been read, far more by nostalgic adults than by children. It is a series of school stories, clearly based on Kipling's days at USC (with Kipling himself nicknamed "Beetle"), but romanticized to the extent that the exploits of Stalky and his two companions are considerably more heroic and successful than those of the trio Kipling belonged to. The school, too, is glamorized. Its headmaster, for instance, is a godlike figure, revered not least for his legendary prowess with the cane—something Cormell Price seldom if ever used. But in this way Kipling is able to sanctify much of the school's incidental and far from godlike brutality, transmuting it into a necessary and admirable part of a necessary and admirable training for life. Alternatively, it becomes one huge joke, as when the headmaster attempts to flog the whole senior school for their insolence in cheering (and continuing to cheer, even as he flogs them) a carefully concealed act of singular heroism he performed during an outbreak of diphtheria.

Perhaps the most intriguing story, from the pen of this laureate of imperialism, is "The Flag of their Country." In it a visiting member of Parliament outrages the boys by addressing them on "Patriotism."

In a raucous voice, he cried aloud little matters, like the hope of Honour and the dream of Glory, that boys do not discuss even with their most intimate equals, cheerfully assuming that, till he spoke, they had never considered these possibilities. He pointed them to shining goals, with fingers which smudged out all radiance on all horizons. He profaned the most secret places of their souls with outcries and gesticulations. (18:256)

At the climax of his peroration, he reaches inside his coat and produces a flag, which he waves at them and waits for the "thunder of applause that should crown his effort."

They looked in silence. They had certainly seen the thing before .... But the College never displayed it; it was no part of the scheme of their lives; the Head had never alluded to it; their fathers had not declared it unto them. It was a matter shut up, sacred and apart. What, in the name of everything caddish, was he driving at, who waved that horror before their eyes? Happy thought! Perhaps he was drunk. (18:257–58)

The key word, of course, is "caddish." The man proved himself to be no gentleman. And so, from time to time, though for the most part preserving the obligatory offhanded reticence on such matters, did Kipling—never quite the insider.

The stories are chiefly important for their celebration of what, in Kipling, is always the necessary corollary of the Law: an impudent lawlessness, a taste for practical jokes (especially in pursuit of revenge), a potential for farce. Almost all such law-breakers (Stalky, Mulvaney, Kim) have a healthy respect for the law they defy, and take their punishment like the men they are or hope to become. The stories are chiefly unsatisfactory, not to say distasteful, for a gratuitous emphasis on cruelty and violence. Stalky and his two allies take (and invite us to take) altogether too much pleasure, for instance, in giving a pair of bullies a taste of their own medicine in "The Moral Reformers."

Puck of Pook's Hill and *Rewards and Fairies*

Puck of Pook's Hill and *Rewards and Fairies* were both written during the first decade of the new century, a time when Kipling's view of things was becoming increasingly jaundiced. What the stories themselves chiefly reflect, however, is the increasing pleasure he found in the company of his children, as well as his excitement at exploring both the landscape and the history embodied in it of what had become, in his own words, "my favorite foreign country," England.[7] Old Hobden, the farmhand-poacher who appears in the frames to most of the stories, embodies this sense of history still with us by seeming to have been around for as long as any of the historical characters we meet.

The format for both books is the same. A brother and sister, Dan and Una, unintentionally conjure up Puck on mid-summer eve. They meet him regularly thereafter, and Puck introduces them to a range of historical characters hailing from neolithic times to the early nineteenth century, each with a story to tell. Such a narrative framework has the disadvantage, as Gillian Avery has pointed out, that a child reading these tales must always have one ear in the present, which lessens his or her chances of surrendering to the spell of the past.[8] For the adult reader, however, many of Kipling's most felicitous touches arise from the interaction of past and present. Sometimes Dan and Una grasp what is meant so quickly and intuitively that time is annihilated; sometimes they quite fail to comprehend, so far apart are the worlds Kipling juxtaposes. Such misunderstandings are far fewer in *Puck of Pook's Hill*. This may be due in part to most of the stories' being set in Roman or Norman times when the world was younger and life can more easily be presented as having been a series of simple adventures and straightforward loyalties. Much more important, however, the two main narrators involved—Parnesius, the young, British-born Roman centurion, and Sir Richard, onetime feudal lord of the fields and woods and stream they look out on, listening to his stories—establish a relationship with the two children which, from the outset, is of a kind inconsistent with misunderstanding. In some later instances, so tortuous does Kipling's narrative technique become, this is not the case.

These two groups of stories also provide the book with a natural thematic unity. For the Roman stories are about the end of an era, whereas the Norman ones are about the beginning of a new and richer period of English history. Yet this simple diagrammatic analysis must be qualified to do justice to their richness. For Parnesius is probably the most attractive narrator in either of the books. And the courage, resourcefulness, shrewdness of judgment, and loyal integrity that he and his friend Pertinax exemplify go a long way toward making the dominant tone of the Roman stories a positive one. Maximus, their commander, depletes the force guarding Hadrian's Wall to dangerously low levels to further his eventually disastrous ambition to be emperor. And they, as a result, having been given effective command of the whole Wall, must placate the Picts by wisely tolerant policies, must conceal their weakness from marauding Norsemen for as long as possible, and must in the end fight on, apparently hopelessly, to the last. Yet they are loyal to Maximus throughout, never once questioning his right to demand such service of them. Their young shoulders carry wise but never cynical heads; their youth enables them and the young reader to snatch a kind of autumnal glory from the autumnal corruption of a dying empire.

And for the adult reader, Parnesius and Pertinax are the unmistakable successors to (or precursors of) Kipling's idealized subalterns in the Indian army, contending not only with the problems of commanding native troops and of handling the local situation on a political as well as a military level, but also with the military and political shortsightedness of their superiors. Similarly, Maximus's irresponsibility in leaving Britain inadequately guarded is just too close to the policies, as Kipling perceived them, of Britain's leaders at the turn of the century for the parallel to be unintended. It is of the fall of more than one empire that Kipling is writing in these stories; more than one "Wall" has been left inadequately defended.

Yet if the stories are about the fall of more than one empire, this must imply the rise also of successive empires. Equally, if the Norman stories are about a new beginning under William the Conqueror, they are also about the defeat of Harold—Harold, who had repulsed a massive Norwegian invasion at the other end of his kingdom only weeks before, and who so nearly defeated William at Hastings. Kipling knew that any English child reading of the last successful invasion of Britain would wish that victory had gone to the loser. So, though the narrator is Sir Richard, knighted by William on the eve of the battle, he must share the stories that show him growing older and wiser with a Saxon companion. More than once, indeed, Sir Richard owes his life and his good fortune to Hugh, the man whom he defeats in hand-to-hand combat at the outset, and whose land he takes, but whose friendship he wins, whose sister he marries, whose land (or its equivalent, further up the valley) is restored to him, and who becomes a Saxon knight, vassal of a wise Norman lord. We are given, in fact, an abridged and highly idealized cameo of the melding of two races that it took several generations and much bloodshed to accomplish.

Subsequent stories in *Puck of Pook's Hill* tell of Sir Hugh and Sir Richard as allies against a further threatened invasion from Normandy, of Sir Hugh and Sir Richard as old men bringing treasure back from Africa, and finally of Kadmiel the Jew, having discovered their treasure years later, sinking it fathoms deep in the sea so as to deny it to King John and help force him to sign Magna Carta. Kipling is often, and sometimes rightly, accused of anti-Semitism. This very story, "The Treasure and the Law," is not free from its taint. Yet Kadmiel it is, unsympathetically as Kipling presents him, who brings as the gift of his race to the amalgam which is Britain that most precious of gifts, the Law.

At the end of *Rewards and Fairies*, in "The Tree of Justice," a story which Dan finds to be "like the woods, darker and twistier every minute," Sir Richard and Kipling return to where they began—Saxon against Norman at Hastings. The final tableau is unforgetable. After a day's hunting during which old enmities surface dangerously, Henry I (about to invade Normandy to punish his eldest brother for plotting to seize a throne rightfully his) is confronted by a gaunt, one-eyed Saxon beater in the service of the king's jester, Rahere. The old man has for years been a witless pilgrim, it emerges, between Stamford Bridge (where Harold of England defeated Harald of Norway) and Battle Abbey (where, two weeks later, William defeated Harold). Rahere explains how he made him "his man" to save him from being stoned as a madman claiming to be Harold of England.

To break the silence which follows, King Henry offers the old man wine, and Sir Hugh (convinced earlier in the day that this is indeed his king) bears the empty cup away, "Saxon fashion, upon the knee." Suddenly no further proof seems necessary. Even the king finds himself arguing, defensively, that Edward the Confessor and Harold himself (under duress when shipwrecked and imprisoned) promised William the English throne. Rahere reminds the king that his brother Robert, too, was promised a throne. Sir Hugh can bear it no longer.

> "Ah, Rahere," cried Hugh, "why has thou shown him thus? Better have let him die than shame him—and me!"
> "Shame thee!" said the King. "Would any baron of mine kneel to me if I were witless, discrowned, and alone, and Harold had my throne?" (25:368–69)

By the end of the story it is everyone else present who has been shamed by Rahere into admitting that not one of them mocks his man, and Harold dies happy.

The tale is told, as becomes increasingly common with Kipling, largely through dialogue and therefore somewhat obliquely. For most readers it will require a second or third reading for all the implications to become clear. But others in the collection are even more opaque, and sometimes much less rewarding, for readers with no more knowledge and experience of life than a child is likely to possess. "The Knife and the Naked Chalk," for instance, tells of a Stone Age man of the Downs who sacrifices an eye to purchase knives from the forest-dwelling workers of metal, and thereby save his people from the wolves their stone weapons are little use against. But he finds himself, as a result, venerated as a god and denied the chance of a wife, children, and the usual human consolations. "Marklake Witches," told by Philadelphia, an early nineteenth-century girl little older than Una, is described by Lord Birkenhead as a "delightful" story.[9] And so it is, in a way, for the adult reader; certainly it is a very deft piece of work, full of dramatic irony. Its charm or pathos depends on the narrator's clearly suffering from consumption, yet not realizing this, and totally misunderstanding, as she recounts it, the behavior this prompts in everyone around her. Adults may find both pathos and comedy when the men in the story are willing to fight duels over her, or are moved to tears by what she takes to be her artistry when she sings a particularly sad song about the brevity of life. But Una is as much in the dark as Philadelphia, as will most child readers be. As for "The Wrong Thing," the corresponding story heard by Dan but not his sister, the whole thing turns on a matter of aesthetics, and takes the form of a conversation between two adults, which Dan overhears but from which he is excluded periodically by knowing laughter. Children enjoy hearing real adult conversations they do not wholly understand, but not reading about them, surely, in stories supposedly written for their benefit.

In far too many of the stories, in fact, one or other or both of the listening children fail to grasp some key or trivial point—such as the fact that the narrator in "Gloriana" is Gloriana herself, though she claims merely to have known the queen; or for what reason unknown to the narrator of "A Doctor of Medicine" the killing, on purely astrological grounds, of all the rats in a plague-stricken village halts the disease; or why Puck waits, in "The Conversion of St. Wilfred," for the saintly archbishop to invite him into the church where he kneels praying; or what it is about the death of Sir Francis Drake's friend Doughty that Puck does not want them to hear in "Simple Simon." In *Puck of Pook's Hill*, if the children do not understand, Puck explains—that, for instance, for Parnesius to meet Pertinax at the Bull Killing is like meeting him in church. The adult reader can still smile, finding a further layer of meaning. But when the children are left in a state of puzzled ignorance, or just ignorant without knowing there is anything to be ignorant about, then Kipling has ceased writing truly for children and is using the genre of children's story as a literary device. As with the chorus in *Murder in the Cathedral*, one of Dan and Una's chief functions comes to be to flatter the readers on their perceptiveness.

Whether the stories in *Rewards and Fairies* were ever popular with young readers is something about which, it will be apparent,

I am in considerable doubt. What I am in no doubt about is that
they are not popular today. *The Jungle Books* and *Just So Stories*
can still be enjoyed by preteenagers who are not all that different
from previous generations of their age. But *Rewards and Fairies*
is just not accessible to readers below the age at which there has
been a profound shift in reading tastes, as well as much else.
Childish things must be put away, it seems, between the ages of
twelve or thirteen and sixteen or seventeen. Historical fantasy is
out; romantic realism, varied perhaps by a dash of the occult, is in.
At the age when fantasy is readmissible, moreover, it must be
total fantasy—Tolkien or nothing. Perhaps we should take
Kipling literally at his word when he says that *Rewards and
Fairies* is "for grown-ups." Certainly, for those adults who can
accept or ignore the frames, there are a number of stories of
charm ("Marklake Witches," "The Conversion of St. Wilfrid")
and power ("The Knife and the Naked Chalk," "The Tree of
Justice").

As for those few children who are interested in historical
fiction, the best two stories in the book—"Brother Square Toes"
and its sequel, "A Priest in Spite of Himself"—are the American
ones. Their bilingual narrator-protagonist, of Anglo-French
smuggling stock, finds himself as a boy an inadvertent stowaway
on the ship carrying a new ambassador from republican France to
the republican United States. The two stories contain a great deal
of action, a good deal of lively history and some even more lively
speculation, a gallery of boldly drawn characters (including
Washington, Talleyrand, and Napoleon), and some obviously
nostalgic descriptions of American scenery and seasons. Mercifully there is a minimum of mystification. If the reader fails to
understand why Talleyrand refers to certain characters as Can-
dide, Dr. Pangloss, and Mlle Cunégonde, the loss is not great.
Finally, in a book where the quality of the poems Kipling was by
now in the habit of placing at the beginning and/or end of his
stories is higher than average, Washington is paid the compliment of being the implied model for far and away Kipling's
best-known poem, "If."[10]

Kipling's best fiction for children, it has been argued, is seldom an oversimplification of life. Almost always there is a richness and a complexity to the vision it offers. In the *Just So Stories* this makes possible an experience truly shared between adult reader and child listener, each enjoying a single story which contrives to be two somewhat different stories. In *The Jungle Books* such complexity consists of different levels of significance to many of the incidents, not all of which are apparent to all readers, certain of which will never be apparent to certain readers, a few of which will be apparent to very few. Yet this in no way prevents each story from being a rewarding and in some sense total experience at each such level of comprehension. Finally, in *Puck of Pook's Hill* and more particularly in *Rewards and Fairies*, complexity and richness begin to be matters of mere literary technique rather than of literary vision. This obsession with what can sometimes be a rather arid exercise of skill is something we shall also observe in Kipling's adult fiction. Noel Annan has described Kipling as "the Regius Professor of the voulu,"[11] and it is precisely this reliance on contrived complexity rather than on a less conscious welling up of richness from levels of the imagination not always at an author's controlled beck and call which marks off *Rewards and Fairies* from *The Jungle Books* and *Kim*. Kipling himself, while describing in detail how he achieved his effects in the former, merely claimed on behalf of the latter two that "My Daemon was with me."[12]

Chapter Four
The Light that Failed

The title of this chapter is a gross oversimplification of what happened to Kipling's non-Indian, adult fiction during the period it covers, from his return to England in 1889 to the death of his son in 1915. As will become apparent, the light burned as brightly as ever in many of the stories he wrote over these years. Nevertheless, the tag is justified to the extent that, between the brilliant promise of his early work, culminating in *Kim* and the other Indian stories he wrote after his return to England, and the astonishingly luminous work to be found in his last two collections, there is an interregnum when both subject matter and quality are very mixed. It seems as if Kipling had to search more assiduously for his raw material in the life he was then in process of living than when in India. It is also clear that some of the dissatisfactions of that life are reflected in his fiction, without in all cases being transmuted into art.

The first work to be considered was something of a false start. For, at the same time as he was continuing to reap his Indian harvest in the 1890s, producing such masterpieces as "Without Benefit of Clergy" and "On Greenhow Hill," he was also writing his first novel, *The Light that Failed*. The work is unique for Kipling in being clearly and fairly intimately autobiographical. To what extent he was influenced in this by the writers around him he so affected to despise, attempting as it were to beat them at their own game, it is impossible to say. Leading the rather solitary life he did, probably the only non-Indian experience he had accumulated in sufficient quantity to form the basis of a novel, at which he was clearly ambitious to try his hand, was highly personal.

Kipling makes a painter of his young hero, Dick—a fairly transparent disguise even from the outset. For we first meet him as an orphaned schoolboy, boarded in a seaside home unmistakably modeled on "The House of Desolation," with Maisie, a girl in similar circumstances, as his companion. The two of them are much older than Kipling was during the Southsea years, but this merely serves to telescope two autobiographical sources of the story. For, during a return visit to Southsea as a schoolboy at USC, to see his sister (who continued to live with Mrs. Holloway for a number of years), Kipling had met and fallen in love with Flo Garrard, his replacement in the household. He wrote poems and letters to her until after his arrival in India, and then ran into her again in the street on his return to London. But she was too absorbed in painting what Trix later described as "her very ineffective little pictures"[1] to respond. Kipling even pursued her to Paris, all to no avail. Hence a good deal of the misogyny in *The Light that Failed*, as well as the account of Dick's development as an artist and of his theories about the nature of art, reflects fairly closely Kipling's own life and feelings at this time.

We next meet Dick, years later, on the banks of the Nile. He has had some formal art training, but has picked up most of what he knows direct from life in the course of roaming the globe. His latest job is as artist war correspondent in the campaign to relieve Gordon at Khartoum, from which he returns to England to find his work the latest rage. His fellow war-correspondent friends are disturbed by his growing arrogance, and attempt to save him from prostituting his gifts, which are for an uncompromising realism, by pandering cynically to the more delicate tastes of a public he despises. In the midst of all this, he meets Maisie again, by chance. She is also an artist, living on a £300 yearly legacy, studying for part of the year in France, and obsessively working at "her very ineffective little pictures." Despite her warnings, Dick assumes that he has only to persevere and she will devolve from artist to artist's wife. So he helps her with her painting every Sunday afternoon. But Maisie meant what she said; she is interested in him only as a tutor. Dick begins to fall into a noticeable decline. Meanwhile stormclouds are gathering, and the war correspondents prepare for their next assignment. Dick rescues his closest friend and neighbor, Torpenhow, from the clutches of a designing young woman, Bessie, only to find he is going blind from a wound received in the Sudan campaign.

In the short time left him, Dick paints his masterpiece, for which Bessie acts as a resentful model. Falling asleep as soon as it is finished, he wakes up blind, so never sees how the vengeful Bessie has destroyed the painting before taking her leave. Desperate to find someone else to care for Dick, Torpenhow pursues Maisie to France. She returns to England with him, but is clearly unwilling to become Dick's keeper and makes good her escape. Dick reassures Torpenhow that she will return next day, however, and packs him off to the new Sudan campaign. After a week or two of mere existence, fed by his miserly landlady, Dick is taken in hand by the still scheming Bessie. Then, one day, she cannot avoid confessing to her vindictive act of destruction. This jolts Dick into taking charge of his life again. With great ingenuity he contrives to travel to Egypt, and finally to make his way to the besieged redoubt in which Torpenhow is covering the fighting—where, of course, he is killed. "His luck had held to the last, even to the crowning mercy of a kindly bullet through the head" (9:329).

At least, that is how the story finally appeared. An earlier, much shorter version, first published in *Lippincott's Magazine*, had Maisie do the right thing by her faithful Dick. Discussions as to whether the shorter version was expanded, or the longer one abridged (the latter seems more likely—a cynical catering to the public's presumed taste to rival Dick's prettying up of his soldiers in action) are of less interest than that both endings are almost equally bad.

In considering why, it may be helpful to differentiate, as Kinkead-Weekes has done, among the three different kinds of light that fail in the book.[2] There is, first, the light of love. The only real flash we see of this is in the first chapter, when Dick and Maisie are incongruously (yet characteristically) tasting forbidden fruit by firing a revolver on the shore.

She stood close to Dick as he loaded the revolver for the last time and fired over the sea with a vague notion at the back of his head that he was protecting Maisie from all the evils in the world. A puddle far across the mud caught the last rays of the sun and turned into a wrathful red disc. (9:13)

Later in the book, Dick's continuing infatuation is hard to credit, not just because Maisie becomes such a shadowy, bloodless creation, but because the emotional ties between him and such male friends as Torpenhow are so much more warmly portrayed than anything he feels for Maisie. As for the much-praised passage when Dick remembers painting his first, lost masterpiece, this does little to suspend our disbelief in his capacity for a hopeless passion. The picture was a mural of sea-devils and sea-angels fighting over a soul, painted in the empty hold of an unseaworthy cargo vessel, with only three colors of paint available, and the mistress ("a sort of Negroid-Jewess-Cuban; with morals to match") of a murderously jealous captain acting as model for devils, angels, and soul alike. "Just three colours . . . , and the sea outside and unlimited love-making inside and the fear of death atop of everything else, O Lord!" (9:151). Woman as devil and angel, as unholy trinity of Afro-Semitic-Latin sexuality, and as source of an ever-present threat of death: what more could one expect, asks Kinkead-Weekes, of an adolescent fantasy?[3] Clearly a concept of love as anemic or as melodramatically wooden as these two extremes could not lead up, convincingly, to an ending where Maisie keeps house for poor blinded Dick. Love has no option but to fail; Kipling and Dick have no option but the theatrical conclusion of the longer version.

The second light is that of art, first seen in Madame Binat's establishment, where

naked Zanzibari girls danced furiously by the light of kerosene lamps. Binat sat upon a chair and stared with eyes that saw nothing, till the whirl of the dance and the clanging of the rattling piano stole into the drink that took the place of blood in his veins, and his face glistened. Dick took him by the chin brutally and turned that face to the light. (9:37)

Binat, the failed artist, stares with figuratively unseeing eyes as Dick draws his face; Kipling's fear of failure—every artist's fear of the sudden drying up of inspiration—is symbolized even more brutally in Dick's literal blindness. Yet even before this, as he explores both his love for Maisie and his need of art, Dick has found himself in the dilemma that the former will not cure him of the insecurity and wanderlust that feed the latter, but that the latter is no substitute for the anchor of a stable human relationship such as he seeks with Maisie.

The final light seems to be an attempt to resolve the twin failures of love and art. The key passage, by coming immediately after the battle where Dick receives the wound that leads to his eventual blindness, and by referring to the opening scene by the seashore, seeks to link them in some presumably significant fashion.

Beyond the lines of the dead, a broad bloodstained Arab spear cast aside in the retreat lay across a stump of scrub, and beyond this again the illimitable dark levels of the desert. The sun caught the steel and turned it into a savage red disk.... Dick raised his revolver and pointed towards the desert. His eye was held by the red splash in the distance, and the clamour about him seemed to die down to a very far-away whisper, like the whisper of a level sea. There was the revolver and the red light, ... exactly as had fallen somewhere before,—probably in a past life. (9:31–32)

Less directly, the scene is linked to Dick's final death in the desert, and also to all the other instances of brute, physical violence throughout the book, such as the immediately preceding battle scene. This is a brilliant instance of Kipling's ability to evoke the integral and unavoidable brutality of much of man's life on earth. Kipling's gift, in this respect, is like Dick's, and to raise objections is to be like those of Dick's customers who prefer their dying soldiers to wear clean uniforms and well-shined boots.

In the description of Torpenhow's desperate unarmed combat with an Arab who penetrates the square, however, such details as his gouging an eye out and then wiping his thumb on his trousers verge on that kind of gratuitous relishing of the finer points of violence which too often disfigures Kipling's writing. Nor has he finished with the incident. Dick recalls it, after his blindness. "D'you remember that nigger you gouged in the square? Pity you didn't keep the odd eye. It would have been useful. Any letters for me?" (9:217). Incredibly, moreover, the intended effect is not to underline Dick's insensitivity but to enlist our sympathy for the stoically stiff-upper-lip way he is taking it all. Perhaps even more distasteful, however, is the earlier scene of suppressed violence where Dick walks around and around the captive newspaper publisher who had intended cheating him of all his war pictures, pawing the fat, unhealthy body he disdains to hit while Torpenhow recovers the sketches. If, in Torpenhow's defeat of the Arab, Kipling seems concerned to prove that mere reporters can be as brutal as anyone else, here he is clearly describing what he would have liked to do to those who pirated his work.

This third light is presumably the escape into the world of action from Dick's mutually exclusive and equally unsuccessful attempts to find himself through art and through love. Yet over and above Kipling's insensitive treatment, for purely personal reasons, of the element of violence, the ending of the story rings ludicrously hollow. "It was a lark, though. I only wish it had lasted twice as long. How superb it must have looked from the outside!" (9:318-19) says Dick, sighing regretfully, after a ride to the front in an armored train under attack. And as he approaches the final redoubt, he exclaims: "What luck! What stupendous and imperial luck!... It's 'just before the battle, mother.' Oh, God has been good to me!" (9:327-28). What, apart from anything else, is Dick's final solution other than a more grandiose, less honest version of the suicide he earlier rejected? Even the light that was meant to succeed fails.

And so, as he himself came to recognize, had Kipling's one excursion into extended autobiographical fiction. The genre required a steadier, more sustained act of introspective honesty than Kipling seemed willing to undertake, even in his autobiography. Dick's blindness is made to symbolize the failure of the outer world to provide the artist with further inspiration. There remains, however, an inner blindness, of which we, the readers, are uneasily aware but of which Kipling seems not to be. The book is in dire need of an ironically detached view either by the protagonist of himself or by the author of his protagonist. What we have is an external mode of narration, as used by Rider Haggard, and by Kipling with much more subtlety than Haggard, applied to an internal, Proustian or Jamesian theme. And since the internal sureness of touch of such authors is lacking, the result is internal melodrama which culminates (though showing little of Kipling's usual sureness of touch with things external) in external melodrama.

Pyecroft and the World of Comedy

For the future, all of Kipling's successes, with the exception of *Kim*, would continue to be in the short story and in poetry. To a much greater extent than might at first be apparent, moreover, the lines along which he would develop the short story had already been laid down in his Indian stories, and would continue to be present in his children's fiction. He had by no means done with India, of course, when *The Light that Failed* was first published. And even when he stopped writing directly about the subcontinent, he kept his lines of communication open with the world of colonial administration in such African stories as "Little Foxes" and "A Deal in Cotton." But clearly the subject matter of his stories changed as his life-style and surroundings changed. Part of the uneven quality of his writing during this middle period may even be attributed to his uncertainty as to where to pitch his tent. Much more potent factors, however, were his disappointment over what happened in South Africa, his disillusionment with his fellow countrymen, and his increasing ideological isolation. Continuity with his early fiction is maintained much more through sustained emphasis on such unchanging human characteristics and preoccupations as laughter, revenge, work, and sorrow, and through further development of well-tried fictional techniques.

One of the most obvious instances of this is the replacement of Private Mulvaney by Petty Officer Pyecroft in a series of stories which take place afloat and ashore. In some of these the old format of the "I" narrator recording what is told him is carried to new levels of complexity; in others, the narrator is observer of and participant in Pyecroft's adventures and misadventures as they befall him; in most, totally new heights of farcial unlikelihood are achieved. In "The Bonds of Discipline," for instance, the narrator has stumbled on a report by a French lieutenant of an extraordinary two days he spent as a stowaway aboard a British man-of-war. So Pyecroft supplies him with an account of what really happened.[4] The "spy" having quickly been discovered and recognized as such, the whole ship's company stages a performance for his benefit. This includes a perpetually drunken captain, a breakdown of the engines, a reversion to improvised sails, and a mock execution "on the foc'sle" for climax. In "The Horse Marines," by contrast, Pyecroft is on shore leave. Here he reduces a large-scale military exercise to a shambles when the two "armies" engage in unofficial but all too real hand-to-hand combat over a child's rockinghorse. (The epigraph quotes Question Time in the House of Commons concerning the use of wooden horses on rockers to teach cavalry recruits to ride.) Both these tales are recounted by Pyecroft in his inimitable way. In "Their Lawful Occasions" the narrator joins Pyecroft and company aboard No. 267 torpedo boat for naval maneuvers, and even takes a hand in their spoiling role when they masquerade as a member of the opposing fleet. As becomes increasingly Kipling's practice, however, much of the story is told through conversation, and much of the conversation is Pyecroft's.

Pyecroft's mode of address does not place him geographically (as with Mulvaney or Learoyd) so much as socially: lower middle (uncle a greengrocer) verging on upper working class, but with pretensions above his station. Hence the dog Latin and puppy French, and the rococo embellishments. "We then proceeded *ong automobile*," he explains in "The Horse Marines," describing their search for a suitably prominent point on which to display the rockinghorse,

along the ridge in a westerly direction towards the miniature fort which had been so kindly revealed by the searchlight, but which on inspection

(your Mr. Leggat bumped into an outlyin' reef of it) proved to be a
wurzel-clump; *c'est-a-dire*, a parallelogrammatic pile of about three
million mangold-wurzels, brought up there for the sheep, I s'pose. On
all sides, excep' the one we'd come by, the ground fell away moderately
quick, and down at the bottom there was a large camp lit up an' full of
harsh words of command. (26:371)

The convolutions of Pyecroft's prose style are matched by
those of Kipling's narrative strategy, and there is a real danger
sometimes that the story line will be lost. This for those who are
not Kipling addicts, and more particularly for those who do not
respond to his love of climactic, almost orgasmal humor, makes
the Pyecroft stories merely tiresome. Moreover, there is little
attempt to create a credible, rounded character out of the protagonist, and still less to balance the comedy with suggestions of the
somber side of his life, such as are found in "The Courting of
Dinah Shadd" and "Black Jack." With one exception, Pyecroft
remains a one-dimensional device for the recounting of uproar-
iously comic extravaganzas.

The exception is the enigmatic "Mrs. Bathurst," where the
narration is shared by Pyecroft and his friend Sergeant Prichard
of the marines, prompted and interrupted by questions and
comments from the narrator and his friend Inspector Hooper of
the Cape Government Railways in South Africa. After some talk
of desertion for the sake of love, which "takes 'em at all ages," the
story centers on Warrant Officer Vickers, who quit with only
eighteen months to go to his discharge. Mrs. Bathurst, the
woman in the case, is a youngish widow who kept a hotel in New
Zealand. She is described at length by Prichard as unremarkable
yet somehow unforgettable. Pyecroft then recounts how Vickeιʝ
dragged him ashore every night of a week they spent in Cape
Town to watch an early movie of shots from real life all over the
globe, including one in which Mrs. Bathurst could clearly be seen
arriving by the Plymouth express at Paddington Station, London,
and looking around her as if searching for someone. Each time
Vickers was highly agitated, even guilty, certain that he was the
one she was looking for. At the end of the week he was sent

ashore on a mission from which he never returned. Before leaving, however, he informed Pyecroft, cryptically, that he was not a murderer, his wife having died in childbirth six weeks after he set sail on his current tour of duty. The story ends with Hooper recounting how he came across the charred bodies of two tramps struck by lightning in a siding far to the north, one of whom can now be identified as that of Vickers from a still discernible tatoo and from two surviving false teeth.

Even from such an account it is clear that many questions are left unanswered. The setting in which the story is told, the conversation which precedes it, the songs sung by nearby pic-nickers, all serve to reinforce the sense of love's potentially destructive force. But even such a basic question as whether Vickers is destroyed by his passion for Mrs. Bathurst, or Mrs. Bathurst by hers for Vickers, has been a matter of debate since the story first appeared, to say nothing of whether the second tramp can possibly be Mrs. Bathurst (or even, as one commentator suggests, the ghost of Mrs. Bathurst).[5] My own preference would be to assume that Mrs. Bathurst discovered the wife she had not been told of in London, that Vickers realized this and was consumed by guilt, and that the two charred figures are to be seen as symbolic of this mutually destructive passion without our having to assume that the two principals were literally united in death. But altogether too much has clearly been left to guess work.

The story is an early and extreme instance of Kipling's late manner, a notable characteristic of which remains the concision already noted in his earlier work. Kipling's chief weapons of revision, if we are to believe him, were Indian ink and a brush, to remove beyond the possibility of recall any word, sentence or paragraph which was not absolutely necessary.[6] And C. S. Lewis has suggested that "Mrs. Bathurst" suffered from too much Indian ink.[7] Such cryptic economy is one good reason why Kipling's characters are never as fully developed as, for instance, those in D. H. Lawrence's short stories. But he is not, in any case, as interested in probing their innermost motivation or states of mind. Nor does he, in anything later than the Simla and Mulva-ney stories, explore a recurring social setting and its effects on his characters, as Lawrence does in his stories of mining communities. Kipling's method is almost the exact opposite, in fact. From largely external evidence in the form of conversation, events we witness or are told about, suggestive or symbolic details such as the words of the picnickers' song in "Mrs. Bathurst," and enigmatic clues, as when Hooper keeps fingering his pocket without ever actually producing Vickers's false teeth, we deduce the course of past or present events. For there is always a plot to what Kipling tells us. In many ways, such as their reliance on dialogue rather than straight narration, on symbol, on suggestion, Kipling's later stories are surprisingly modern. Yet they never become, as do Katherine Mansfield's, mere impressionistic slices of life. Something always happens, or has happened. In an increasing number of cases the plot consists of unraveling a mystery as to what has happened ("Mrs. Bathurst," "The House Surgeon," "The Madonna of the Trenches," "The Gardener") or what is happening ("Wireless," "They," "Beauty Spots," "Unprofessional") or both ("The Dog Hervey," "Fairy-Kist").

"Mrs. Bathurst," then, is just too enigmatic to arouse any emotion other than bewilderment or frustration. For the most part, however, Pyecroft's world is one of pure laughter. And laughter as a purging, resolving, redeeming factor is an increasingly important feature of Kipling's fiction at this time. There had been comedy, of course, in earlier stories such as "The Three Musketeers" and "The Rout of the White Hussars." And in the later stories, where other avenues to healing and restoration are explored, laughter remains important. But, during these middle years, laughter seems to provide Kipling with almost his major source of release from the pressures one senses were building up as a result of his political and other frustrations.

Sometimes comedy comes in its pure form, insulated within a story which may be juxtaposed with others of darker tones but which contains no hint of these within itself. Of this kind are such Pyecroft escapades as "Their Lawful Occasions" and "The Horse Marines." So, also, is "My Sunday at Home," even though the series of incredible coincidences, with increasingly farcical consequences, reminds one of the existence of the somber merely by being so obvious a parody of Hardy's narrative mechanisms. Touched by malice, but only lightly so, are stories such as "Brugglesmith," "The Puzzler," and "The Vortex," either because the victims deserve their fate or because their social standing adds such piquancy to their discomfiture. The best example of Kipling's consciously presenting laughter as a cureall is probably "The Honours of War." Three subalterns are in deep trouble through ragging a rather serious-minded colleague with a wealthy barrister for a father. Colonel Corkran (Stalky), the Infant (from "A Conference of the Powers"), now middle-aged, and the narrator (Beetle) rescue the victim from a sack in the back of the offenders' car, wine and dine him, sympathize with his indignation and his determination to take the matter as high as the War Office if need be, and finally, when he is shown his three tormentors asleep upstairs, help him with the sudden, irresistible urge he feels to tie them up, dress them as young women, and transport them to the officers' mess as prize exhibits. For this reader, Kipling's blatant antiintellectualism mars the story but does not wholly preclude his enjoying its high spirits.

All laughter is potentially punitive, of course, and though it is so often restorative in Kipling, it can also be highly vindictive. The gales of laughter which, at the end of "Little Foxes," greet the visiting radical politician when he tries to reassure the natives in their own tongue that he will protect them from their colonial masters, unaware that a crucial word in his rote-learned speech is inappropriately taboo, are Kipling's revenge on all such busybodies. And in "The Village that Voted the Earth was Flat," the vengeance of ridicule engineered by leading figures in the press, the theater, and politics, all of whom have been victimized by a motorist-hating magistrate, is totally disproportionate. The final scene of high farce in the House of Commons, though a release of sorts, is also the culmination of a process which, initiated by the laughter-makers, takes on a monstrous and terrifying life of its own.

Most of Kipling's uproarious comedies, whether innocent or vindictive, are curious instances of art used with great skill for lowbrow ends. There is something as essentially juvenile as what

celebrants after a football victory get up to—in a word, of sheer
animal high spirits—about most of them. Significantly, women
hardly figure in them at all. Perhaps the dichotomy between man
of action and man of letters is more completely resolved in these
stories than in any others. Understandably, therefore, they have
done little to enhance Kipling's reputation with intellectual readers. Nevertheless, the best of them are in some ways Kipling's
most singular contribution to the art of fiction.

"Mary Postgate" and Revenge

Not all the revenge stories for which Kipling is so notorious
end in laughter, of course. Curiously, however, the volumes of
this middle period are relatively free of pure revenge stories,
despite Kipling's bitterness during the Boer War and in the years
following. The one notable exception before the 1914–18 war is
the brilliantly angry "A Sahibs' War." This is narrated by a Sikh
warrant officer who has accompanied his young English lieutenant on extended sick leave from India to see some action in South
Africa. Able to say things it would not be seemly to hear from
English lips, Umr Singh can voice Kipling's own frustration at
fighting a war with people who can claim civilian status in the
morning and take their guns out of hiding in the afternoon. The
story is told after the lieutenant, fighting with an Australian
battalion, has been shot from a house where he has just been
shown permits certifying the civilian status of all within. Heart-
broken, Umr Singh and a Pathan who has joined forces with him
await their opportunity for revenge. In the end, as they are about
to hang the occupants of the house, the lieutenant's ghost forbids
them to participate thus in what is "a Sahibs' war." But it is far
from clear that Kipling sides with the ghost rather than Umr
Singh. We may not agree with or respect Kipling's point of view
on the South African War, but we must respect his ability to
create a narrator who can so persuasively and so passionately tell
a story from that point of view.

For examples of wartime revenge carried out in full we must
turn to two stories written in 1915. "Sea Constables" tells of

reserve naval officers using their own boats to shadow a "neutral"[8] oil tanker whose skipper wishes to sell to the Germans. After days of this cat-and-mouse game the neutral skipper falls ill, puts in at a remote Irish port to surrender his cargo, and asks to be run over to London to see his doctor. The officer who has been following him politely declines and leaves him to die. "If he'd been a wounded belligerent, I might have taken him aboard ...; but as it was, he was a neutral—altogether outside the game."

Very much part of the "game," however, is the German airman the middle-aged Mary Postgate watches die. Spinster companion to the elderly Miss Fowler, whose orphaned and unprepossessing nephew, Wynn, she helped rear from boyhood, she has not long ago heard of his death while training to be an airman. She has also (and here Kipling loads the dice a little unfairly) just seen the body of a child killed by a bomb dropped in the village, from which she was returning with paraffin to help burn all Wynn's personal belongings.

The shrubbery was filling with twilight by the time she had completed her arrangements and sprinkled the sacrificial oil. As she lit the match that would burn her heart to ashes, she heard a groan or a grunt behind the dense Portugal laurels. (26:507)

By the light of the bonfire she makes out the badly wounded body of the German airman. So she brings Wynn's revolver from the house and waits for the intruder to die. "A man, at such a crisis, would be what Wynn called a 'sportsman' "; what she was doing was "woman's work."

She ceased to think. She gave herself up to feel. Her long pleasure was broken by a sound that she had waited for in agony several times in her life. She leaned forward and listened, smiling. There could be no mistake. She closed her eyes and drank it in. Once it ceased abruptly.

"Go on," she murmured, half aloud. "That isn't the end."

Then the end came very distinctly in a lull between two rain-gusts. Mary Postgate drew her breath short between her teeth and shivered from head to foot. "*That's* all right," said she contentedly, and went up

to the house, where she scandalised the whole routine by taking a
luxurious hot bath before tea, and came down looking, as Miss Fowler
said when she saw her lying all relaxed on the other sofa, "quite
handsome!" (26:513)

"Sea Constables," by contrast, is innocently straightforward:
those who are not for us are against us and inasmuch as they are
indifferent to our fate (or even make a profit out of it), we shall be
indifferent to theirs. But "Mary Postgate," though it may have
begun as a simple "they also serve who only sit and hate" piece of
propaganda, turns into a terrifying anatomy of that hatred. (It
also, surely, shows how deep-rooted Kipling's fearful conviction
must have been, from childhood, that "the female of the species is
more deadly than the male.") We are compelled to acknowledge
what we would very much rather avoid having to acknowledge:
that the most unlikely of us is capable of unspeakable acts of
cruelty. True, on rereading the last few pages of the story, we can
recognize a forced quality to some of the writing ("the match that
would burn her heart to ashes"), and a gratuitously salacious
dwelling on certain details, even to the orgasmal shudder at the
climax of Mary's love offering to Wynn. But Kipling's very use of
such strong sexual overtones, found nowhere else in his writings,
coupled with the heroine's final, hideous transfiguration to
beauty, suggests that the story took charge, as it were, and wrote
itself. In its envoy, "The Beginnings," Kipling can muse, from the
detachment of his study:

> It was not part of their blood,
>   It came to them very late
> With long arrears to make good,
>   When the English began to hate.
>   (26:515)

But in the story itself we watch an elderly virgin in such matters
raped by that hatred—and, what is worse, enjoying it. Whatever
Kipling thought he was writing, what he actually wrote is a
cautionary tale in which what the Germans do to Mary Postgate is
far more horrifying than what they do to the child they kill.

Parables, Politics, and Technology

Evil in "Mary Postgate" is translated into but not transformed by art. That Kipling was able to do the latter toward the end of his life, in works it is not entirely impertinent to mention in the same breath as *A Winter's Tale* or *The Tempest*, will become apparent. But the years between the Boer War and the First World War were the lean years of political isolation and of a number of stories whose sterile bitterness reflects Kipling's mood. "The Army of a Dream" is an extended piece of rather desperate wishful thinking about the future, in which the English have become enthusiasts about matters military, completing their training in drill while still at school, competing with one another for the limited number of places in the regular army, and as civilians happily serving several weeks a year in the militia. Equally but more negatively didactic, "Below the Mill Dam" and "The Mother Hive" are both fables. In the former the rat and the cat speak with the voices of traditional, precedent-bound England. They refuse to listen when the waters tell them that they come from new streams, diverted to increase the flow. They are doomed, however, when somewhat to its surprise the wheel finds itself turning an electric generator which floods the old mill with light. Kipling's conservatism is of a thoroughly up-to-date, antipicturesque kind when he chooses. "The Mother Hive," by contrast, is Kipling's bitterest attack on debilitating socialism, as preached by the wax-moth, whose caterpillars riddle the whole structure of a hive too effete to guard against such an enemy. The message is much the same as in the earlier "A Walking Delegate," written while Kipling was still living in America. Both stories reveal the essentially Protestant or Carlylean work ethic that underlies Kipling's political views. The chief defect of socialism is that it makes people lazy. Both stories also reveal how simplistic Kipling's view of things can become when he reduces them to a diagram or a parable. In most of his other fiction (even in such other political fiction as "As Easy as A.B.C.," and almost above all in the best of his children's fiction), he knows much better than that. But once he dons his polemic hat, he no longer knows, it seems, that he knows any better.

Others of his animal stories and fables, such as "The Maltese Cat," are more readable. But this did not prevent that aristocrat of the New World, Henry James, from affecting to be rather scornful of the way Kipling's fictional characters kept falling in the social scale.

> ... he has come down steadily from the simple in subject to the more simple—from the Anglo-Indians to the natives, from the natives to the Tommies, from the Tommies to the quadrupeds, from the quadrupeds to the fish, and from the fish to the engines and screws.[9]

Since James had earlier praised Kipling's stories about private soldiers (Tommies) more highly than any of his other Indian stories, what prompted the amused outburst was presumably the appearance of ".007" and "The Ship that Found Herself." In the first case a shedful of railroad engines, and in the second the various parts of a ship on her maiden voyage, conduct lengthy conversations with each other. And it does come as a surprise that the author of "Black Jack," "The Courting of Dinah Shadd," and "On Greenhow Hill" (to name only three of the "Tommy" stories praised by James) could write such crudely anthropomorphic and simplistically didactic pieces. It indicates, I think, a certain lack of concern on Kipling's part for the dignity of his calling—a lack of concern arising from a scale of priorities which too often saw art as the handmaid rather than the source of what truth he had to impart, as a means to an end rather than an end in itself.

In this case, however, as well as being fables carrying a typical Kipling moral, the stories are examples of the increasing fascination the art of the engineer came to have for him. This is evident from "The Bridge-Builders" onward, and is epitomized in those two Scottish ship's engineers, McAndrew (of the poem "McAndrew's Hymn") and McPhee. The best story in which the latter appears, "Bread upon the Waters," is ostensibly a revenge story. But its real emphasis is on the fierce pride of an engineer for whom the safety of the ship is of first importance. This is contrasted with his former employers' willingness to cut corners for the sake of profit, which in the end gives McPhee the sweet satisfaction of towing one of their ships back into port. In a curiously similar way, though "The Devil and the Deep Sea" ends with a crew of smugglers sinking their crippled vessel just where a pursuing customs ship will break her back on the wreck, the major part of the story is about how, against all the odds, they patch her up so as to escape from the Asian port where they are being held captive. All other considerations, whether revenge or the ethics of smuggling, are subservient in these stories to the pride of a craftsman who is at the same time a man of action.

Given this interest on Kipling's part in technology, his two ventures into science fiction should come as less of a surprise than they sometimes do. In "With the Night Mail" Kipling holds our interest mainly at a technological level. What is chiefly fascinating is to note those respects in which Kipling is right and those in which he is wrong, in this "Story of A.D. 2000," written in 1905, about future transatlantic flight. Its sequel, "As Easy as A.B.C.," however, constitutes the most enigmatic, the most intriguing, and in my view the most profound statement he ever made of a political nature. It also shows how much more pessimistic he had become, between 1905 and 1912, about the ease with which man's future could be assured by the application of technology and a little common sense.

"The A.B.C." (Aerial Board of Control), explains the narrator of "With the Night Mail" in a passage which serves as epigraph to the later story,

that semi-elected, semi-nominated body of a few score of persons of both sexes, controls this planet. "Transportation is Civilization," our motto runs. Theoretically, we do what we please so long as we do not interfere with the traffic *and all it implies*. Practically, the A.B.C. confirms or annuls all international arrangements and, to judge from its last report, finds our tolerant, humorous, lazy little planet only too ready to shift the whole burden of public administration on its shoulders. (24:148)

The planet Kipling describes "has had her dose of popular government. She suffers from inherited agoraphobia, She has no...use for Crowds" (26:7). Her inhabitants live very much to themselves, the ultimate offenses being "crowd making" and "invasion of privacy." And it is a case of these two that the A.B.C. is called on to attend to in Chicago.

When the four deputed members of the board arrive there, accompanied by the whole war fleet (whose commander is pathetically grateful for the chance of a real full-scale exercise), they discover that the local authorities are scarcely able to contain the anger of what amounts to a crowd (though a crowd horrified to discover that this is what it has become). This anger is directed at agitators who are trying to turn it into a full-blooded, old-fashioned crowd, demanding political rights. The board restores order, stunning the crowd with intense light and then intense sound from the entire fleet. But still, when they land, they find the inhabitants (particularly the women) so enraged at this attempt to take them back to the bad old days that one of them tries to commit suicide in protest. They demand to be taken over and ruled directly by the board, to ensure an end to the threat of Democracy, and the board accedes reluctantly, its first administrative act being to load the agitators aboard the flagship for safe keeping. Then the problem becomes what to do with them. On the return journey, however, a solution is discovered. London, it seems, is more tolerant of amusing eccentrics than Chicago. One of the city's chief impresarios agrees, over the radio, to take the prisoners off the board's hands and put them on display. There they will be able to make speeches and vote and be democratic to their hearts' content, watched by an incredulously curious crowd.

On the surface we are presented with Kipling's version of Utopia: a docile population which has rejected democracy and demands nothing more than efficient, authoritarian government, and a benevolent, technocratic dictatorship which supplies this somewhat reluctantly. (As with most utopias, psychological credibility is a tiresome irrelevance.) Yet, as in Swift's Houyhnhnm society, there are more than a few hints that perfection has gone too far. The Mayor of Chicago, for instance, seems almost to appreciate the agitators when he bemoans the impossibility of getting any response from the normal citizenry as to the quality of government he provides, just so long as it's not democratic. And De Forrest of the board ruefully agrees. Reluctantly, Kipling seems to be admitting that, whatever the faults of the democratic form of society he so justifiably castigates, the cure—any cure, even a cure made to order—may well be worse than the disease.

Healing and the Supernatural

Kipling's fascination with technology gives rise to another remarkable story, "Wireless," whose real focus of interest might seem anything but technological, but which succeeds largely because it captures so well the sense of mystery surrounding radio in its early days, just as "Mrs. Bathurst" exploits the miracle of cinema. In the back room of a drugstore the owner's nephew, young Mr. Cashell, is trying to make contact with another pioneer of radio. In the drugstore itself the narrator talks to the druggist or "apothecary." An attractive young girl comes in and, the narrator having agreed to look after the shop for half an hour, drags the coughing druggist out into the bitterly cold night for a walk "round by St. Agnes." Left to himself, the narrator concocts an exotic, mildly alcoholic drink. Shaynor, the druggist, returns, coughs (the narrator glimpses blood on his handkerchief), writes some letters, then drinks what the narrator offers him (commenting on the bubbles around the brim, "like a string of pearls winking at you"), and falls asleep. The lights shining through the colored bottles, falling on the picture of a girl (remarkably like Shaynor's) in a toothpaste advertisement, and the blue spiraling fumes from a pastille burning just below the poster to relieve the druggist's cough, create an appropriate atmosphere for what is to come.

The narrator chats to the radio operator awhile, understanding little of what he says, but grasping some notion of "induction." Then he hears Shaynor talking, and finds him in a kind of trance, reciting and writing down imperfect versions of lines from "The Eve of St. Agnes." Eventually Shaynor wakes, and reveals by his answers to veiled questions that he has never heard of Keats, still less read him. At the end of the story Cashell has been unable to contact his fellow operator; he and the narrator eavesdrop, however, on two ships unable to reach each other satisfactorily, but both of whose signals they can hear perfectly.

While listening to Shaynor's garbled Keats, the narrator naturally speculates on possible explanations, dwelling on all the other coincidental similarities. But the effect is to make us realize that any attempt to rationalize this analogous form of "induction" will fall short of a satisfactory explanation. The mystery of how the lines came to Shaynor is as impenetrable as that of how they came to Keats in the first place. All his life Kipling was intermittently drawn to the supernatural as subject matter, but never did he use it more tactfully and suggestively than in "Wireless" and that neighboring masterpiece in *Traffics and Discoveries*, "They."

This story takes as its starting point Kipling's experiences as a motorist, and the countryside the car enabled him to explore. One day, at the opposite end of the county, the narrator explores a long road, dwindling to a path, through the woods, and finds himself on the lawn of a secluded Jacobean mansion, an armed topiary knight's green spear at his breast. The house and the garden are full of strange, elusive children whom the blind woman who owns the place is surprised he can see—something she has never been able to do. He travels from "the other side of the county" to pay several further visits, on one occasion using his car to bring medical help to a child in the village who, the next time he calls, is dead. Always the children are there, yet, shyly, not there. On the final visit, having driven through fog to get there, he meets a village woman hand in hand with a child in the woods. She tells him his is in the house. Still, as on each of the previous occasions, talking to a blind woman whose house is full of children who are not hers, he fails to understand. She, on the other hand, understands him uncannily—knows, when a surge of anger at an instance of cruelty she recounts fills his mind, that the colors of his thoughts are ugly.

I was silent, reviewing that inexhaustible matter—the more than inherited (since it *is* also carefully taught) brutality of the Christian peoples, beside which the mere heathendom of the West Coast nigger is clean and restrained. It led me a long distance into myself. (22:353)

Suddenly, in the middle of this serene story, we are reminded of Kipling's brutality in other stories, and of a small child experiencing and learning brutality at the hands of an earnest Christian woman with whom he must live for five long years.

On this final visit the children are particularly elusive, always in the next room as, for the first time, he is shown over the house. But he senses at last, as he and his guide sit by the fire, which he stirs with a faggot, there being no iron near the hearth, that they are behind a screen in back of his chair. So, while the blind woman sees through the attempts of a surly tenant to outwit her, he lets his hand hang loose and feels it held for a moment, long enough for a kiss to brush the palm. Suddenly, without looking, he understands. And when he takes his leave, and explains he will not be coming back, his hostess understands that, though it is right for her who has never had children of her own, and right for some who have had children, it would not be right for him.

This story is extraordinarily rich—richer even than "Wireless," with all its Keatsian paraphernalia—in symbolic or suggestive details: the repetitive insistence that the narrator is from "the other side of the county," the yew spear at his breast, the fog hindering his final visit, the lack of iron by the hearth, the blind woman who sees so much more than he does. Whether more quickly and intuitively than the narrator or not, it is entirely through touches such as these that we penetrate the mystery about which Kipling is so reticent.

After his son's death, in 1915, Kipling came under considerable pressure from his sister to attempt psychic communication with John, but always he refused. Angus Wilson thinks this was because Kipling had no intimations of an existence after death, still less any firm belief in such. He therefore finds the ending to "They" dishonest, as well as unsatisfactory in that it leaves us so mystified as to why it would be wrong for the narrator to return.[10] For myself, I would not presume to call in question Kipling's right, in this his first and only attempt to give artistic form to his grief at Josephine's death, to leave unstated his narrator's reasons for not coming back, any more than I would query his own motives for not exploiting such emotions in any further stories. Clearly, in saying this, I am implying that the story need not be taken as being about reunion of an exclusively psychic nature. But if and to the extent that it is, we should perhaps remember that Wordsworth did not need to believe, literally, in Plato's myth of preexistence to be able to use it to express what he felt to be profoundly true.

An underlying theme of the story is clearly that of healing, and this takes place all the more easily against a background of the English countryside at its best—may even to some extent be brought about by that background. This theme will become increasingly important in Kipling's writing, but is present intermittently throughout this troubled period of his life. The healing power of laughter has already been touched on. Less exuberantly, "An Habitation Enforced" tells of a rich American taking a rest cure in the English countryside on doctor's orders. Its effectiveness is greatly increased when he and his wife buy and restore a crumbling old mansion, assume the almost feudal responsibilities for their tenants that go along with the building, and are accepted as the rightful heirs to the status enjoyed in local society by the wife's forebears before they emigrated to America. How can any healing take place if one has no useful function, and if one does not belong? "The House Surgeon" is about the laying of a ghost in an otherwise charming old house when a former owner is disabused of her shameful conviction that her sister committed suicide while living there. And in "My Son's Wife" a young intellectual, Frankwell Midmore, is "cured" of his fashionable left-wing views, and the friends that go with them, by inheriting a country property and gradually becoming more and more involved in its upkeep and the affairs of his new neighbors.

Water plays an important part in this and other stories—a violent, cleansing part. For the flooding of the stream that runs through Midmore's property sweeps away some lingering pretenses as well as precipitating the final stage in his cure. Newly harnessed water power is used, as we have seen, to help sweep aside outdated attitudes in "Below the Mill Dam." And finally, in "Friendly Brook," water performs a rather gruesome act of healing when another flooded stream drowns a blackmailer from the city. This grim little masterpiece, with vignettes of country folk at work which recall the ever-present Hobden of the Puck stories, seems to unite in a single work the revengeful and the restorative aspects to Kipling's work. For, though the blackmailer's victim in no way seeks to bring about the drowning, he is grateful for the relief it affords his family, and philosophically recovers the latest installment of tribute money from the dead man's pocket before launching the corpse once more on the rising waters. Then, in the spirit of that timeless heathendom one finds in rural communities, he is content to allow the stream to carry away his haystack. "The Brook had changed her note again. It sounded as though she were mumbling something soft" (26:72). The story might almost, one feels, have been written by Hardy.

The Children of the Zodiac

Perhaps the feature which has emerged most clearly in this study of Kipling's middle period is the great variety of stories he wrote. To take but one collection (and not his most diverse), *Traffics and Discoveries*, there are three stories from the war in South Africa, "The Captive" and "The Comprehension of Private Copper" having a good deal of political content, and "A Sahibs' War" being a grim tale of arrested revenge. Then there is the shallow double-length politico-military fantasy "The Army of a Dream," and the bitter political fable "Below the Mill Dam." Interspersed with these are Kipling's first four Pyecroft stories, which range from the farce-fantasy of "The Bonds of Discipline" to the enigmatic "Mrs. Bathurst." Finally there are those two fine but very different experiments in the supernatural, "Wireless" and "They."

It is difficult in some ways to credit that "A Sahibs' War," "Their Lawful Occasions," and "They" could have been written by the same author, and the same author, moreover, who also wrote ".007," "Mary Postgate," "As Easy as A.B.C.," and "The Children of the Zodiac." And yet, on examining this last-named, early story, first published the year after *The Light that Failed*, one realizes how, like "Friendly Brook" but far more comprehensively, it incorporates many of the facets and features of its author's past and future work and thus reflects a unity of sorts underlying all this apparent diversity. It is, in the first place, a fable, or rather, a myth—a deeply serious Just So Story. It tells of gods—and in particular of a god and a goddess, Leo and Virgo—who begin by thinking of themselves as immortal, and who therefore cannot understand human tears and human laughter. Gradually, however, it is borne in on them that they too will die, and like Krishna in "The Bridge-Builders" they learn to weep and to laugh in sympathy with men and woman. They experience the balm of laughter, like Mulvaney and Pyecroft, and they discover, as Ameer and John do in "Without Benefit of Clergy," that death teaches them how to love. They find, too, like McPhee and Findlayson, that work of one kind or another, and pride in work well done, helps them forget that death may strike at any time. Leo even learns to sing, as Dick in *The Light that Failed* wants to learn to paint, so that others may learn to forget death, and so that men and women may one day become worthy successors to the gods.

So completely have Leo and Virgo come to share our humanity by the end of the story, moreover, that their concern for what happens to others is matched by our concern for what happens to them. As a result the story becomes one of the few in the Kipling *oeuvre*—one of the very few in this middle period of his writing—in which we glimpse the abyss that some of his characters sense below their feet. An abyss of sorts there surely is in "Mary Postgate," but it is we rather than the woman on its brink who experience the horror. An abyss there may be beyond the enigma of "Mrs. Bathurst," but is is veiled in obscurity. Only in "The Disturber of the Traffic," written in the same year (1891) as "The Children of the Zodiac," does the Kipling of the middle period, arguably still writing in the manner of the early period, provide us with an equally chilling sense of the abyss.[11] But its lighthouse-keeper protagonist, even lonelier than Hummil in "At the End of the Passage," retreats from his warped awareness of it into mercifully simple-minded forgetfulness. Leo and Virgo, on the other hand, like Findlayson and Mulvaney and Ameera and John, discover that whatever positive quality life possesses depends on the attempt to combat and alleviate, in oneself and for others, the nihilism and despair that gazing into the abyss induces. As Alan Sandison points out,[12] if much of Kipling's imperialistic and political propaganda (whether as in "The Head of the District," or as in "The Mother Hive") had been presented less as the complete solution it clearly was not, and more as merely another interim (and more or less desperate) measure to cope with chaos and darkness, he might not have aroused the antagonism he did.

Finally, "The Children of the Zodiac" throws perhaps the clearest light of any story of his on the debatable nature of Kipling's religious beliefs. The one thing that is agreed on is that Kipling was in favor of religion, in the same way as he was in favor of law, irrespective of what might be perceived by this or that observer to be the merits of this or that particular religion. Religious truth was always more a matter for Kipling of what exists because people believe in it than of what people believe in because it exists. It was a necessary embodiment of their fears and hopes, as well as offering, like Masonry, "an average plan of life"—"what everybody knows ought to be done."[13] For this reason he did not approve of the activities of missionaries. "The matter of creeds is like horseflesh ...," says Mahbub Ali. "Therefore I say in my heart the Faiths are like the horses. Each has merit in its own country" (19:234–35). Moreover, argues Kipling in his own voice, "when man has come to the turnstiles of Night all creeds in the world seem to him wonderfully alike and colourless."[14] Or, as he paraphrases Horace (5.22):

> Glazed snow beneath the moon;
>   The surge of storm-bowed trees—
> The Caesars perished soon,
>   And Rome Herself. But these

> Endure while Empires fall
> And Gods for Gods make room....
> Which greater God than all
> Imposed the amazing doom?[15]

The question, then, comes down to which greater God—if any.
All the gods of all the religions, as Kipling reminds Christians
scornful of idolatory, are made in the image of man.[16] Are they no
more? Does Kipling, for instance, use an approximately Christian God, in "Recessional," much as I take him to use astrology in
"Unprofessional," reincarnation in "The Finest Story in the
World," psychic communication with the dead in "They," psychic
telepathy in "Wireless," or an old wives' tale in "The Wish
House," as pure myth to express what are probably aspects of
essentially human experience which we cannot understand or
readily express in any other way? Such a view is certainly the
easier to reconcile with "The Children of the Zodiac," as it is with
"The Bridge-Builders." Or does he regard the Gods as genuine
intuitions, however crude, of a genuinely superhuman order of
existence which we are even less capable of understanding?

The answers to such questions may not have been known with
any greater certainty by Kipling than by his critics. My own
inclination is to side with Alan Sandison, Elliot Gilbert, and
Angus Wilson, rather than with Bonomy Dobrée and J. M. S.
Tomkins, and take the former view. But such verdicts, either way,
probably owe more to the reader's own beliefs than to evidence
supplied by Kipling. And in the end it makes very little difference. Whether it be a "greater God" or merely an "ultimate
reality" that informs Kipling's credo, He/it is so far beyond
man's understanding as to offer little reassurance to the individual that his or her particular concerns weigh much amid the broad
cosmic matters that must be attended to. The abyss at our feet
may well be as real and as terrifying in the one case as in the other.

In the end, however, it must be admitted that the attempt to
find the unity of this middle period in "The Children of the
Zodiac" is less than satisfactory. The story itself comes so early in
the period, and so many of the stories whose themes or character-

istics it subsumes are even earlier. The Indian stories can be seen, when viewed as a whole, as a search for some kind of equilibrium. And the children's stories seem to have their unifying paradox of complexity within simplicity. But the very variety, range, and unevenness of theme and treatment which prevent the stories of the middle period from having any discernible unity are what in fact characterize them. This may merely indicate that the notion of a single "middle period," lasting much longer than those which precede and follow it, and overlapping with both to some extent, is at best unilluminating and at worst untenable. Yet in a sense this middle period is more characteristic of Kipling than any other through its very diversity and apparent lack of unity. T. S. Eliot says of his poetry, and might with equal justice have said of his prose:

Now one of the problems which arise concerning Kipling is related to that skill of craftsmanship which seems to enable him to pass from form to form, though always in an identifiable idiom, and from subject to subject, so that we are aware of no inner compulsion to write about this rather than that—a versatility which may make us suspect him of being no more than a performer.... We expect to feel, with a great writer, that he *had* to write about the subject he took, and in that way. With no writer of equal eminence to Kipling is this inner compulsion, this unity in variety more difficult to discern.[17]

The one obvious unifying factor is a compelling need for diversity. The reasons for this we shall in due course return to; its most tangible and probably most important result is Kipling's lifelong preference for the short story.

Chapter Five
Limits and Renewals

Even the titles of Kipling's last two collections of stories, *Debits and Credits* and *Limits and Renewals*, suggest a kind of taking stock or balancing of the books. Such would not be surprising in these products of his final period. And indeed we find many of the old themes and preoccupations and approaches reappearing. "Aunt Ellen" is a kind of apotheosis of his farcial motoring stories; "A Naval Mutiny" is a seafaring comedy with ornithological embellishments; "The Debt" has an English child listening to the talk of Indian servants. Laughter, revenge, and healing are probably the most persistent continuing themes from his earlier work. But in most cases we do not feel, reading these new stories, that Kipling is perfunctorily or wearily going over old ground. For the limits, though acknowledged, are pushed back, and the renewals are not just a matter of sewing on patches, but include some restyling. In particular, while the best of the stories in these collections are clearly by the same hand that wrote the best from previous collections—a hand that has lost none of its cunning in the interim—the head and the heart guiding that hand are a little wiser and more compassionate.

Of the twenty-eight stories under consideration, thirteen are about the war or its immediate aftermath. The subject broods over the collections like the Angel of Death's wings in "On the Gate" and "Uncovenanted Mercies." Not surprisingly, some of them are revenge stories. But none is remotely as disturbing as "Mary Postgate," and in no case is vengeance directed at the Germans. In "Sea Constables," as we have seen, an unscrupulous neutral gets what he deserves; in "The Tie" and "A Friend of the Family" sundry old scores against war profiteers are paid off; while in "Beauty Spots" the climax is a typical Kipling orgy of comic revenge. Yet, though this is masterminded by a survivor of wartime gas attacks, and has as its victim a retired Regular Army major who has probably never fired at anything more dangerous than a partridge, but who seeks a quarrel with his new neighbors, the irony is not exploited—except, belatedly, in the poem which follows. The various strands to the story are only coincidentally linked, and there is no strong unifying theme.

The element of convalescence or healing in "Beauty Spots" is found in many more of these postwar stories than that of revenge. Sometimes the cure is only partial, as in "Fairy-Kist," or left in doubt, as in "A Madonna of the Trenches"; sometimes it seems complete, as in "The Woman in His Life." Sometimes the victim must go through a reenactment of whatever it is that haunts him. So, in the last-named story, when the young bitch John Marden has come to love is trapped in a badger's set, and he must rescue her, he has to face all his accumulated horror at being in a confined space underground, after years spent undermining enemy trenches. Sometimes, as in the other two, it is enough to recapitulate the experience verbally. But most of all, healing depends on a return to the familiar, to routine and ritual. So Wollin in "Fairy-Kist" thankfully resumes his gardening. So Humberstall in "The Janeites," even after being medically discharged as a case of shell-shock, returns to his front-line unit and is kept on as officers' mess waiter. So Faith and Works 5837, a Masonic Lodge in London, opens its doors in "In the Interests of the Brethren" to any soldier on leave or in hospital who can show a minimum familiarity with Masonic ceremonial, and is always crowded. "All ritual is fortifying. Ritual's a necessity for mankind. The more things are upset, the more they fly to it," says Brother Burgess. "I abhor slovenly ritual anywhere," he adds. And then, as if to make it clear that what he and Kipling have in mind is not the dead hand of stultifying ritual, he asks the narrator, "By the way, would you mind assisting at the examinations, if there are many Visiting Brothers to-night? You'll find some of 'em very rusty but—it's the Spirit, not the Letter, that giveth life" (31:68).

Too many of such stories, however, show the same lack of focus noted in "Beauty Spots." In "A Madonna of the Trenches," for instance, a young soldier is brought to admit that the memory haunting him is not that of the corpses under the duck-boards,

creaking like leather when they froze, but of his sergeant, whom
he had known all his life, committing suicide. This took place
after the two of them saw the ghost of the young soldier's aunt,
whom the older man had loved for years, it emerges, even though
she was married to another man, and of whose death from cancer
the young soldier would receive word a few days later. So what is
really troubling him, he now maintains, is doubt as to the true
nature of things. "If the dead *do* rise—and I saw 'em—why—why
anything can 'appen." Yet it is far from clear that this self-
diagnosis is any more to be trusted than the previous one. His
greatest horror seems reserved, rather, for the fact that these two
old people should have been in love for so long without his
realizing it, and should be so greedy to spend eternity together.

"For I saw 'er," he repeated. "I saw 'im an' 'er—she dead since mornin'
time, an' he killin' 'imself before my livin' eyes so's to carry on with 'er
for all Eternity—an' she 'oldin' out 'er arms for it!" (31:281)

He may claim that he can no longer marry his onetime fiancée
because she does not have the same look on her face as his
aunt—that look which is for all eternity. But we may suspect that
what he really cannot bear is the thought of never knowing for
whom she is reserving such a look. We are left wondering
whether the story is about a capacity for heavenly or an incapacity
for earthly love.

   This lack of a single theme or focus is something Angus
Wilson detects in all the Masonic stories.[1] And to the extent that
he is right, this is probably because the narrator is so clearly none
other than Kipling, and Kipling is so clearly indulging himself on
some favorite topics, whether the rituals of pipe-smoking,
Masonic regalia and ritual, Jane Austen, or ghosts. If these were
the first stories that a purchaser of *Debits and Credits* in 1926
happened to light on, he or she might well have felt that Kipling
was beginning to lose his grip. Knowing what is still to come, we
can see that, in all these direct accounts of their experiences by
survivors of Ypres, the Somme, and Vimy Ridge, Kipling was
merely resuming the healing rituals of writing after the death of

his son. Not very noteworthy in themselves, the stories are a necessary preliminary. Fiction is still being written today about the Western Front, by people who were not even alive when it all happened. The world is still trying to come to terms with the first of this century's holocausts. Kipling would not do so until he was able to transpose the raw events into a different key and setting, and find the right musical forms in "The Gardener," "The Church that Was at Antioch," and "The Wish House."

Much the most spectacular cure of a war casualty—indeed, a miraculous cure—is described by an old French soldier turned curé in "The Miracle of St. Jubanus." As a boy, Martin Ballart had been a typically mischievous acolyte with "the eyes of a joyous faithful dog, and the laugh of Pan himself" (33:351). But he returned from the war a morose, withdrawn automaton, with no more interest in the fiancée who had once delighted him than in anything else. Until, that is, the curé prayed in desperation to his church's patron saint, also an old soldier, whose sole recorded miracle had been to restore a dead man to life and laughter by whispering a joke in his ear. The following Sunday two of a new generation of mischievous acolytes, together with the local schoolmaster and skeptic, became accidentally attached to the curé's umbrella, left open to dry in the vestiary, and performed a weird ballet around the church, reducing priest and congregation alike to helpless laughter in which even Martin was finally caught up. This, of course, released him from his nightmare. But the curé took things a step further. By extemporizing on the virtues of laughter and on the miraculous cure it had effected, and by praising the noble part played in all this by the humiliated teacher, he turned the poor man into the hero of the hour and achieved a second miracle in the form of his conversion.

The story is far from as side-splitting an experience for the reader as the best of the Pyecroft or Stalky tales. We believe in the laughter of others, but the purely visual experience which prompted it cannot involve us, through the mere printed word, in the same way as the rage of cavalrymen confronted with a child's rockinghorse. The laughter, moreover, is so benign. Nobody is humiliated. Comedy has, for once, been purged of any taint of the punitive—is so health-giving as almost to cease being funny. Almost, but not quite. For, in this his final protestation of faith in the sovereign power of laughter, expressing itself in a kind of grotesque delight at a silent trio pirouetting, not over an engulfing abyss but under the shadow of an engulfing wave of mirth, Kipling does not allow either his dancers or his readers altogether to lose touch with the earth. This is farce striving, not unworthily if not entirely successfully, to achieve the status of Arnold's "high seriousness." This is Pyecroft among the angels.

Healing and Forgiveness

"The Tender Achilles," which recounts the only remaining wartime cure to be considered, is also the first of a group of stories in which Kipling once more revels in the expertise of experts, those inner circles of which he loved to grant himself honorary membership. Wilkett, a brilliant medical research scientist and a perfectionist, is luxuriating in self-pity after the war, plagued by guilty memories of all those occasions when, as a merely average surgeon at the front line, he had done less than might conceivably have been done for his constant stream of patients. He is also suffering from a slight but persistently infected wound in his foot. So, since nothing else will cure him of the perfectionism that feeds his guilt, his colleagues falsely diagnose the wound to be tubercular, and operate to remove part of the heel. Such a mistake, made when there are none of the pressures of war to excuse it, so infuriates him when he learns of it that his guilt evaporates and he hobbles back to his research. A cunning ruse has cured him of the symptoms, but the surgery has not touched the root cause of his breakdown—his infernal pride. Perhaps too much of what his colleagues value in him depends on that Achilles heel.

"Unprofessional" is also about doctors—a rather less orthodox group, as the title implies, who discover that the normal tissues of the body respond to cosmic influences in what are termed "tides," whereas cancerous tissues remain unaffected. They find that mice, and humans, benefit much more from treatment which is synchronized with such tides. Then they stumble on the remarkable fact that mice, and humans, when cured by such methods, attempt to commit suicide at about the time they would have died if left untreated. As one woman patient expresses it, "I ought to be busy dying." What might have been an eerily compelling story, however, provides us with little encouragement to suspend our disbelief. For one thing, having taken a great deal of trouble to persuade us that we are more intricately a part of the workings of the entire universe than we had supposed, Kipling allows his doctors too easy a victory over the cosmos. And for another, there is just too much overt discussion among members of the team, for our benefit as well as each other's, as to what is happening and why. "Wireless," that other Kipling story set on the frontier between science and the occult, retains its sense of mystery by being far more reticent.

By contrast, the next two studies of experts and the mysteries of their craft are among the finest examples of what Kipling can achieve by letting the participants tell their own story. "The Eye of Allah" is set in a medieval monastery well known for the quality of its illuminated manuscripts. John of Burgos, an artist who often works for them, and who for safety and convenience passes as one of their number on his travels, is about to leave for Spain. From Spain he will bring drugs for the monastery's infirmary, the raw materials out of which the rarest colors can be pounded and ground, and new ideas and sketches for all the devils in the St. Luke's gospel he is busy illustrating. In Spain there awaits him the mistress—Jewish or Moorish?—who is clearly the model for the Virgin we watch him painting. Kipling is at his deft best in the conversations through which we become conversant with the mysteries of medieval book production and medicine, and indeed from which we glean almost everything the story has to tell us, without any character seeming to stop and explain what his ostensible listener would have been well aware of.

Twenty months later John is back, the mistress having died giving birth to a dead son, and begins to learn that for grief such as his "there is, outside God's Grace, but one drug," as the abbot phrases it, "and that is a man's craft, learning, or other helpful motion of his own mind" (31:403). Some months later he surfaces from his labors, to be invited to dinner by the abbot. At the table also are Roger de Salerno, an Italian physician attending the

abbot's lady, Friar Roger Bacon, and Brother Thomas, the infir-
marian. The conversation turns to the causes of disease and
Brother Thomas confesses himself "at a loss unless—as Varro
saith in his *De Re Rustica*—certain small animals which the eye
cannot follow enter the body by the nose and mouth, and set up
grave diseases. On the other hand, this is not in Scripture"
(31:412). The two Rogers find themselves in immediate agreement that always having the Church restrict their speculations
thus is an intolerable restraint on men of learning. At this point
the abbot, despite having taken off his ring of authority at the
beginning of the discussion, tactfully asks John to show them
some of the devils he has drawn for his Luke. The assembled
doctors are astounded. But they are even more so when, the abbot
having recalled how the Saracens who once held him prisoner
showed him such creatures in a drop of water, John produces a
primitive microscope and does just that. At first Brother Thomas
is close to breaking point at the thought of these unsuspected
depths to God's creation. Roger de Salerno asks where they stand
if Mother Church hears of their having "spied into Her Hell
without Her leave," and the abbot replies, "At the stake." Roger
Bacon protests that the Pope is wise and learned, that with the aid
of John's instrument he can prove the truth of what he asserts,
that his name weighs with men who dare to think.... "I will not
give this up!" he concludes. But the abbot, having slipped his ring
on his finger again, smashes the dangerous toy with the hilt of a
dagger he borrows from John. Such knowledge is before its time.
"It will," he adds sadly, "be but the mother of more death, more
torture, more division, and greater darkness in this dark age"
(31:428).

The story is almost all mere talk, yet creates a whole gamut of
well-differentiated characters and builds up to a brilliant climax.
It anticipates, by several centuries, the whole Copernicus-Galileo
scenario: theory and hypothesis may be tolerated, but the ability
and the presumption to prove them will not. Moreover, in the
person of John, we have perhaps Kipling's finest portrait of the
artist, and as if in honor of the fact, the prose he writes is like an
illuminated manuscript, full of brilliant detail.[2] Edmund Wilson
and others, including myself, have accused Kipling of being in

some sense ashamed of his calling, of devaluing it by contrast with a vocation to action.[3] Yet stories like this and "The Children of the Zodiac" would seem to belie the charge. John is as involved as any of the characters and more in the joys and sorrows of the world around him, yet his final loyalty is to his art and his final consolation is in his art. Which is why he can be such a detached observer of the scene before him. The destruction of the microscope, and the whole issue of the challenge it offers to the Church's version of truth, leave him untouched. He has used it to see and record his kind of truth, and has no further need of it. Finally, in the death of John's mistress and child, and in the impending death of the abbot's gracious lady, we have a reminder of the inescapable mortality of all human endeavor. This, while not in the least deflecting attention from the main focus of the story, underpins our heightened sense of the excitement and frustrations of human discovery with an awareness of those realities which nothing under the sun, new or old, will change.

Kipling indulges his penchant for having us eavesdrop on the conversations of experts even more freely in "The Manner of Men." The story is ostensibly about St. Paul and the shipwreck on his way to Rome. It is told, years later, by the captain (now harbor inspector at Marseilles) and his second in command on that voyage, in conversation with a young Spanish captain whose ship badly needs "girting" or undergirding. This reminds the inspector of how, on that earlier voyage, he had omitted to take just such a precaution. Yet even before this salty exchange begins, the opening descriptive paragraph sets the professional tone for what is to follow.

Her cinnabar-tinted topsail, nicking the hot blue horizon, showed she was a Spanish wheat-boat hours before she reached Marseilles mole. There, her mainsail brailed itself, a spritsail broke out forward, and a handy driver aft; and she threaded her way through the shipping to her berth at the quay as quietly as a veiled woman slips through a bazaar. (33:241)

Kipling is far from invariably correct when seeming to be knowledgeable, but in this case the sails seem to be much as they might

have been, as indeed are all the other details of nautical equip-
ment and procedure in the story. The only serious error seems to
be that, according to the biblical account, the captain of the ship
carrying Paul did undergird his ship.[4] The purpose of so elaborate
a frame is presumably to let us sense the good opinion these
hardy mariners, whose credentials Kipling is at such pains to
establish, hold of the little "Jew philosopher" they once had as
passenger. But, in fact, Paul is in some danger of being lost sight
of under all the nautical apparatus with which the story is bal-
lasted. In this case the frame almost constitutes the story, which,
since we know the outcome already, may even be Kipling's
intention.

More compelling in many ways is "The Church that Was at
Antioch," in which both St. Paul and St. Peter are upstaged by a
young Roman police officer named Valens. Even more than
Parnesius, Valens recalls those idealized young heroes of the
early stories. He "has all the firmness, tact and tolerance which a
first-class English subaltern might be expected to show in face of
some more or less incomprehensible communal squabble in
British India."[5] For the Syria where he finds himself posted to
serve under his uncle, Sergius, is presented as uncannily like India
under British rule. Substitute, for Hindus and Moslems, Christians of Jewish and Christians of Gentile extraction, engaged in
bitter strife (fanned by agents from the synagogue in Jerusalem)
over such matters as what food is ceremonially fit to be eaten.
Under his uncle's wise tutelage, however, he soon becomes a
shrewd judge of situations. The tone of the story verges, at times,
on the complacent arrogance of the Anglo-Indian, yet is miracu-
lously rescued by Valens himself, who is never quite too good to
be true. (Perhaps the fact that he owns a young slave girl rescues
him from the self-righteousness of a Bobby Wicks or a Brushwood Boy.)

Paul has gone in search of Peter to help resolve the food
disputes, and in his absence Valens narrowly escapes death while
calming an artificially provoked riot. He lets his would-be murderer escape, however, so as not to bring further trouble on the
harassed Christians. Finally, after Paul and a moodily self-

doubting Peter have restored peace to their congregation, Valens is stabbed in a dark alley and dies pleading with his uncle, "Don't be hard on them.... They get worked up.... They don't know what they are doing" (33:121).

The whole story is in fact full of references to the crucifixion. Sergius, in refusing to arrest Paul just because the Jews want him to, adds that "One of our Governors tried that game down-coast—for the sake of peace—some years ago. He didn't get it" (100). Peter, unsure of himself throughout the story, turns on Paul at one point to ask, "Do you *too* twit me with my accent?" (109). Valens's slave girl refers to him, more than once, as "her God who had bought her at a price" (122). Valens impresses Paul early in the story, moreover, by the way he can penetrate through all the superficialities of religion to the heart of the matter. "But—as a servant of Mithras, shall we say—how think you about our food-disputes?" Paul asks him.

"As a servant of Mithras I eat with any initiate, so long as the food is clean," said Valens.

"But," said Petrus, "*that* is the crux."

"Mithras also tells us" Valens went on, "to share a bone covered with dirt, if better cannot be found."

"You observe no difference, then, between peoples at your feasts?" Paulus demanded.

"How dare we? We are all His children. Men make laws. Not Gods," Valens quoted from the old Ritual.

"Say that again, child!"

"Gods do not make laws. They change men's hearts. The rest is the Spirit."

"You heard it, Petrus? You heard that? It is the utter Doctrine itself!" (33:107-108)

But it is Peter who responds, in awe, to the dying words already quoted. "'Forgive them, for they know not what they do.' Heard you *that*, Paulus? He, a heathen and an idolator, said it." Quick to agree, Paul adds, "What hinders now that we should baptize him?" But he has no answer when Peter, finding the authority which has eluded him up to this point, asks quietly, "Think you that one who has spoken Those Words needs such as *we* are to certify him to any God?" (122.)

The story is far from a pious Christian tract. Indeed, Mithraism comes out of it rather better than Christianity, as does Masonry, that other simple soldiers' creed, in other stories. And Valens is more than a match for the two saints. Moreover, Peter's final words express something very close to Kipling's own views on the merits of this form of religion as opposed to that one. The source of the values embodied in the story is much more clearly that line of self-sacrificial devotion to duty one can trace in Kipling's early stories about idealized subalterns and selfless administrators, right on through Parnesius and Pertinax in *Puck of Pook's Hill*, and which here reaches its apotheosis—the man of action who is peacemaker and savior. To have written once more of the self-sacrifical heroism of the British subaltern—of the post-1914 subalterns dying by the thousands in a blood bath to which Kipling must sometimes have felt he had dispatched his only son—would have cut too near the bone. By transposing such heroism to Syria in the first century, however, Kipling can reaffirm, with a deepened understanding of the nature of the task and of the price demanded, all his earlier faith in youth.

It may by this time have struck the reader as just too ridiculous to link the figure of Christ not merely with Valens, as Kipling clearly does, but with such impossibly pink and pukka heroes as Bobby Wicks of "Only a Subaltern" and John Chinn of "The Tomb of His Ancestors." Yet here is part of the exchange between the latter and his commanding officer, just before he sets out, alone, to pacify the rather primitive tribe from which the regiment is recruited. (His grandfather founded the regiment, his father commanded it, and John is regarded as the reincarnation of these two quasi-divinities.)

"You've some kind of hereditary influence with the little chaps, and they may listen to you when a glimpse of our uniforms would drive them wild. You've never been in that part of the world before, have you? Take care they don't send you to your family vault in your youth and innocence. I believe you'll be all right if you can get 'em to listen to you."

"I think so, sir; but if—if they should accidentally put an—make asses of 'emselves—they might, you know—I hope you'll represent that they were only frightened. There isn't an ounce of real vice in 'em, and I should never forgive myself if any one of—of my name got them into trouble." (13:155)

What he says comes as close as can be expected of a self-deprecatory British subaltern, I think, to Valens's paraphrase of Christ's words on the cross.

Vengeance Foresworn, Self-sacrifice Embraced

"The Church that was at Antioch" is a response, I have argued, a positive response to four years during which the nation as a whole, and the Kipling family in particular, lost the flower of its young manhood. Lest some readers should have felt that even such muted optimism was too facile, however, without a more strongly expressed countervailing sense of the darkness that is beyond healing, Kipling supplies such in a very different story of forgiveness. For "Dayspring Mishandled" is also the most deeply laid of all Kipling's revenge stories. Manallace and Castorley are both hack writers in an early literary factory turning out formula novels. Both also love the same woman, who marries someone else and is then deserted by him. Castorley comes into an inheritance and sets himself up as a critic, and eventually as an authority on Chaucer. Manallace continues to live by his pen, and to make enough money to support the deserted woman from the time she begins to show signs of paralysis until she dies. Castorley, however, churlishly refuses to help pay for an operation she needs, writes hostile reviews of Manallace's books, and finally insults the memory of their mutual love in some way which is never divulged (Angus Wilson thinks it must have been an insinuation that her paralysis was the result of syphilis),[6] but which provides Manallace with a new mission in life.

Nothing of his plans is explicitly revealed as yet, but his attempts to make archaic inks, his sitting at Castorley's feet to learn all he can about medieval manuscripts and penmanship, his purchase of a battered Vulgate of 1485, and so forth, make it clear that the discovery of part of a hitherto unknown Canterbury Tale, used as part of the binding of an old Bible, is no accident. Castorley is consulted, of course, and vouches for its authenticity. Manallace even circulates a petition to secure Castorley the knighthood he has always coveted. At this point Manallace reveals to the narrator just how long he has spent laying his trap. Then Castorley falls ill. His wife, moreover, seems determined to put him even more in Manallace's power. It only takes the discovery that she is having an affair with Castorley's doctor to convince Manallace that she knows what his game is, and is hoping that the revelation will kill the poor invalid. The story ends with Manallace protectively thwarting the woman's attempt to hasten what he has spent half a lifetime trying to bring about.

Yet the forgiveness, if that is the right word, is of a singularly hollow kind. Manallace is suddenly enabled to see, in the petty distorting mirror of the wife's active connivance, just how meaningless his revenge would have been. But his actions provide no new meaning to a life which, selflessly devoted for so many years to the protection of another human being, has for so many further years been equally selflessly devoted to the destruction of another human being. "That which is marred at birth Time shall not mend.... / Dayspring mishandled cometh not againe."[7]

The prospect facing Helen Turrel at the end of her story, "The Gardener," is just as bleak, just as empty. This much-praised work of Kipling's ostensibly keeps its secret until the final page. But in fact the hints and clues as to the true state of affairs become broader and broader as the story progresses, and are poignantly clear on a rereading. Not that the pathos derives from a harsh fate such as Hardy would have contrived for one in Helen's position. The tone of the opening paragraphs clearly implies that some of the villagers may have had their doubts in accepting the story of how her brother had married unwisely in India and died shortly after the birth of his son, and of how Helen, in the South of France at the time for her health, had taken delivery of the child in Marseilles and brought him back to England. But such doubts were never voiced. Helen, who is fortunate enough to be financially independent, is therefore able to bring up her "nephew," Michael, in comfort and without stigma.

The pathos, in Kipling's handling of events, lies in the fact that she can never be quite honest with the boy, verbally or emotionally. The pathos lies in the way her grief, when Michael is reported "missing, presumed killed," cannot express itself freely or to the full. The pathos lies in how, when she goes over to France to visit his grave and a woman in the same hotel confesses that the grave she keeps coming back to see is that of a son she cannot acknowledge as hers, Helen will not join her in a common grief. The supreme pathos is that, when she cannot find Michael's grave and a man planting seedlings says, "Come with me, and I will show you where your son lies," she cannot even recognize, let alone accept, what is being offered her, "supposing him to be the gardener."

This seems to me a very subtle story. Its scrupulous reticence is not just a game Kipling plays to keep the reader guessing, but reflects the reticence Helen must observe at all times. Nor does Kipling openly suggest that things could or should be otherwise. The props and proprieties of society, which are clearly important to Kipling, demand for their own self-protection the pretense that they have not been transgressed. And the readiness with which such a pretense is sustained by the villagers is less hypocritical than merciful in a clumsy, shamefacedly human way. To Helen, honesty would certainly have seemed harder, on her child if not also on herself. Yet the need for such prolonged pretense brought with it its own, perhaps greater penalties, not least of which was the inability to respond to a higher kind of mercy.

Kipling's use of the gardener-Christ figure might be thought to raise, once again, his attitude to revealed religion. But it need not be read as more than the symbolic use of a story invested with strong emotional overtones for most of his readers, whether believers or not, to represent the kind of forgiveness or acceptance by another which can precipitate self-forgiveness, self-acceptance. Helen has already shown herself incapable of responding to the needs, and at the same time to the unwitting offer to share her burden, of the woman in the hotel. So the end of the story can be read as showing either that she *is* equally impervious to divine mercy, or that she *would be* if it were offered. This is one of Kipling's most compassionate stories, perhaps because it is also one of his most desolate.

From a story of revenge that suddenly seems empty and gives way to an almost equally empty forgiveness, and one where the central character has concealed her guilt for so long that she is in the end unable to accept her own or anyone else's forgiveness, we turn to the richest of all Kipling's late stories—one in which sickness and healing, forgiveness and self-sacrificial love, are all strands in the stuff of human experience. The evil encountered, the suffering endured, the forgiveness and love offered in response, are all much less heroic than in the case of "The Church that Was at Antioch," since the story is about a very ordinary elderly woman, not a dashing young man. But the result is more rather than less moving.

"The Wish House" is told almost wholly through conversation, which slips in and out of retrospective narrative, as two old women exchange reminiscences. Mrs. (Liz) Fettley (thin, wiry) has made a long bus journey to a Sussex village on one of her increasingly infrequent visits to her childhood friend. Mrs. (Grace) Ashcroft (plump, hampered in her movements by a longstanding ulcer on her shin) is entertaining her. Their opening exchanges set the tone for what is to follow. They compare notes on ungrateful grandchildren ("'No odds 'twixt boys now an' forty year back. 'Take all and give naught—an' we to put up with it! Pore fool we!"). Mrs. Fettley drops a hint that the grandson who puts in a brief appearance reminds her of one of Mrs. Ashcroft's old admirers ("Your Jane never showed it, but— *him*! Why, 'tis Jim Batten and his tricks come to life again"). Mrs. Ashcroft responds tartly, and this prompts a confession from Mrs. Fettley concerning a major infidelity of her own, and one in turn from Mrs. Ashcroft to the effect that neither she nor her husband was beyond reproach in this respect. Indeed, on his death bed he had warned her to beware that no man deal with her as she had dealt with some.

After his death she went to London as a cook-housekeeper, returned to the village while her employers were abroad, and worked on a farm for the fresh air. There, in Harry, she who had always been in control in such relationships met her match. She persuaded him to take work in some London stables for a while. But when he had had enough he returned to the village and to his mother. Her chief withdrawal symptom was splitting headaches, and one day a little housemaid who loved her as a second mother slipped out of the house during one of them, and returned with a headache of her own, Grace's in the meantime having suddenly cured itself. Later the girl told her she had gone to a Wish House—one which has long stood empty and you can ring the bell and ask a spirit to take away the trouble or sickness of a loved one and lay it on you. So, when Harry fell seriously ill, Grace visited the Wish House. That night she cut her shin on the fireplace, and developed a weeping boil which would not heal. Harry, of course, made a miraculous recovery. And for years after that the wound would almost heal and then break out painfully again, responding like a barometer to Harry's health or sickness.

By the time the conversation with Mrs. Fettley is taking place, of course, the wound has turned cancerous and taken on a "life" of its own. Each of the women doubts whether they will ever meet again (which perhaps accounts for their openness with one other), since Mrs. Fettley is going blind and Mrs. Ashcroft feels she will not live to see another "hoppin'."[8] The nurse comes in to dress the wound, and the visitor, glancing quickly at it as bidden, takes her leave.

In introducing the story I referred to the self-sacrificial love it exemplified. But the phrase does less than justice to the fiercely possessive nature of both the love and the sacrifice. Denied any other hold over Harry, Grace derives great satisfaction from how dependent he has been on her without ever suspecting it. When asked what she would do if he married, she thinks she will be spared that. "I reckon my pains 'ull be counted agin that" (31:149). And more than once she insists on being reassured that "The pain *do* count to keep 'Arry—where I want 'im. Say it can't be wasted, like" (31:150).

At no time, of course, are we asked to believe, literally, in wish houses or in physical ailments that drain off another's pain. Grace Ashcroft's own belief is quite enough to account for the persistence of her self-inflicted wound. But her wish to believe and her willingness to undergo all that such a belief entails are the embodiment of an easily recognizable kind of human love. More common in women than in men, since it is so obviously an extension of the self-sacrificial stereotype of maternal protectiveness, it is often far from being an attractive form of love. For in many cases such willingness to undergo suffering on another's behalf seeks not so much to ensure the beloved's well-being as to deny him or her to anyone else. Despite just such a negative quality to what Grace feels and does for Harry, however, she does not put her suffering on display, nor does she use it to exert a kind of moral blackmail. Moreover, this is not her preferred mode of loving. She is driven to it largely because she has so much more to give than he can accept. Of the occasion when her one-time rival for Jim Batten threatened her with a pitchfork, she says, scornfully, "She shruck too much for reel doin's." Grace, by contrast, when she needs an excuse not to return to London so as to spend an extra two weeks with Harry, pours scalding water over her arm.

Harry, on the other hand, leaves her few illusions from the beginning.

"I had signs an' warnings a-plenty; but I took no heed of 'em. For we was burnin' rubbish one day, just when we'd come to know how 'twas with—with both of us. 'Twas early in the year for burnin', an' I said so. 'No!' says he. 'The sooner dat old stuff's off an' done with,' 'e says, 'the better.' 'Is face was harder'n rocks when he spoke." (31:132–33)

And when he has had enough, when he discovers how much more she has to offer than he knows what to do with, he goes back to mother—never, significantly, to look at another woman.

All this wasted richness of emotional response is made the more poignant by the setting and the circumstances in which it is recounted. In many ways the ending of "The Wish House" seems just as bleak as those to "The Gardener" and "Dayspring Mishandled." In all three cases a driving force with an essentially negative end in view, but which has nevertheless given purpose and a sense of direction to an individual's life, peters out in unfulfillment and emptiness. Yet this is to ignore what Grace could have given and wanted to give her man had she been allowed to. If one compares the emotional lives of Helen Turrel and Grace Ashcroft, there is to the latter's love a quality of recklessness, of not counting the cost, which gives just enough of a tragic tone to these closing months of her story to inhibit any condescending pity within such compassion as we feel. Just as when he moved from the world of middle-class Anglo-Indian administrators to that of Mulvaney, a downward shift of class enables Kipling to portray an ability to be in touch and at ease with one's feelings from which, too often, his characters are debarred by the obligatory reticences of their social standing.

The poem preceding this story is of particular interest. A woman has offended a god in some unspecified way, is punished by an incurable, festering wound, and "in Love's honour" remains faithful to her culpable "Vision." "What is a God," asks Kipling in conclusion, "beside Woman? Dust and derision!" With such warrant from the author, it is possible, I think, to see Grace Ashcroft as the incongruously heroic equal of Valens. Lovers of life both, they could not love it half so much loved they not "Love's honour" more.

Finally, the short-story form toward which Kipling is moving in some of the best of these late stories ("The Church that Was at Antioch," "The Manner of Men," "The Eye of Allah") receives its almost perfect expression in "The Wish House." This form consists of more and more being told us, either in retrospect or at the time the events are taking place, in the words of the participants, with narration playing a less and less obtrusive role. In this, of course, Kipling is merely obeying the post-James strictures on the novel to approximate more and more nearly to the state of drama. And in a sense Kipling had always done this in some of his work, whether by letting a participant be principal or sole narrator ("On Greenhow Hill," "A Sahibs' War") or by narrating largely through conversation ("A Conference of the Powers," ".007," "The Tender Achilles"). But the ever-present danger, with Kipling, is that the means of narration will obtrude—that Kipling will enjoy either the back-slapping bonhomie of those assembled ("Slaves of the Lamp," "The Honours of War") or the idiosyncrasies of a narrator such as Pyecroft more than is good for the story. The two old women in "The Wish House," however, begin by establishing the nature of their relationship, and from there slide into Grace's narration, prompted and punctuated by comments from Mrs. Fettley, so easily and naturally that we are entirely drawn into their narrow world for these few pages. When, over halfway through the story, Kipling for the first time offers us half a sentence of interpretive explanation, instead of the barest record of what took place and what was said, we are quite jolted by the change in tone.[9] Frame and narrative, moreover, not only provide an ironic contrast but form a continuous interlocking unity throughout the story.

Late Fables and Parables

First published in *Nash's Magazine* one month after "The Wish House," "The Bull that Thought" is a late fable on a new theme for Kipling. For Apis, the bull, is an artist—an artist in death. We follow his career, as he outthinks the farm boys he butts in the yard, the rival young bulls he kills on the Camargue, and the young men he fights with padded horns in Arles arena, right up to the real thing in a Spanish bull ring. Here he kills his first man, or rather, his first three—mere picadors—before clearing the stage of all other actors, including the visiting star matador. At this point there is nothing further to do except wait for the Civil Guard to shoot him with the guns they are already fingering. Until, that is, an aging mediocre matador named Chisto, who had once been a herdsman and who knows bulls as most matadors do not, steps into the ring. Man and bull weigh each other up, and then put on a performance which holds the crowd spellbound. Chisto is clearly inspired by the occasion, and Apis, who could end the fight at any time he chooses, plays up to him. (His manner changes abruptly when Villamarti, the star matador, reenters the ring and is viciously and unceremoniously chased out again.) Chisto and Apis trust each other and need each other. For, at the end, Chisto walks out of the ring with his arms round the bull's neck, sparing Apis as Apis had spared him.

One's first reaction is that only Kipling would think of representing art in so barbarous a manner. And one's second is that Kipling, like Apis, has merely displayed his techniques; that the story has both advocated and exemplified the virtuoso but sterile exercise of skill and skill alone, such as results in "Mrs. Bathurst," "The Wrong Thing," "Steam Tactics"—and "The Bull that Thought." Yet this is to ignore Chisto, the aging and pedestrian performer who rises to the occasion: "mediocrity itself," as the narrator says, "but, at heart—and it is the heart that conquers always, my friend—at heart an artist" (31:246). It is even to ignore what is said about Apis as artist. "He raged enormously; he feigned defeat; he despaired in statuesque abandon, and thence flashed into fresh paroxysms of wrath—but always with the detachment of the true artist who knows he is but the vessel of an emotion whence others, not he, must drink" (31: 247-48).

That both are described as artists, and that Villamarti too is presumably a kind of artist, need disconcert us only if we insist on allegorizing the story too closely. Fairly clearly Apis is both the embodiment of skill or technique and the factor that inspires Chisto to excel himself. Equally clearly, Chisto provides Apis with a channel or opportunity through which to operate. If we wish to regard man and bull as separate entities, C. A. Bodelsen has pointed out that Apollo was both artist and inspirer of artists.[10] And Kipling himself, though attributing a muselike authority to the activities of his Daemon ("When your Daemon is in charge do not try to think consciously. Drift, wait, and obey" [36:202]), nevertheless instances such specific advice as he received from that source as almost always being of a technical nature. So Apis can be regarded as Apollo/Muse/Daemon, and Chisto as flesh-and-blood artist at heart and of the heart.

Are not all such mythologies, however, attempts to describe the two sides to the artist's head? The essential import of the

story, surely, is that the true work of art, the perfect bull fight
which brings order and beauty to the chaos of mere living and
dying, depends on a partnership or equilibrium between the Apis
and the Chisto within every artist—between skill and feelings,
spirit and clay. . . . But to specify thus is to reduce the story to mere
platitude, whereas in fact it is a fine example of just such a
partnership. For, as Apis and Chisto go through their performance, which ranges from knife-edge grace to sheer buffoonery—
art, yet always only a hair's-breadth from life, or rather,
death—one realizes that nothing less than this particular image,
at first sight so grotesquely inappropriate, will serve to convey
what Kipling wants us to know about the ordeal, and the exhilaration, of creation.

"The Bull that Thought" is perhaps Kipling's most subtle and
successful fable. *Limits and Renewals* ends with a kind of parable
which, if not as successful, is much more ambitious in scope.
"Uncovenanted Mercies" is a story of Heaven and Hell in which
the Archangel of the English overlooks the offenses of two
Guardian Spirits under his jurisdiction in ignoring the Orders of
Life of the two souls they are responsible for, and allowing them
to meet. Such "Oriental flourishes" are out of place and demoded
in today's progressive world, he argues; much more can be
achieved by giving people what they want. He even wonders,
now that his people's standards of comfort have risen, whether
Azrael (Angel of Death) could possibly see his way to mitigate
the crudity of some of his methods and come up with a more
civilized *modus moriendi.* Gabriel and Azrael are rightly scandal-
ized, as is Satan, who was also at the meeting. So the Prince of
Darkness invites the other two to inspect his facilities for reconditioning human souls (often in a sorry state due to angelic
dereliction such as they have just witnessed) into fit material for
Guardian Spirits, and incidentally to follow up the story of the
two souls under discussion.

When they enter the abyss—as, for the first time in his fiction,
Kipling in such stories as "Dayspring Mishandled," "The Gardener," and "The Wish House" does more than glance into its
depths—even "the glare of the halo he [Satan] wore in His Own

Place fought against the Horror of Great Darkness" (33:409). Naturally they discover that the two souls in question (whose Orders for Life predict that, if they ever meet, *"their state at the last shall be such as even Evil itself shall pity"*), having married, are making each other's lives a misery. Yet, when they eventually arrive in Hell and the same trio reassembles to observe them further, they are still clearly in love. Moreover, by invoking a higher authority, the Guardian Spirits, (who, in Kipling's scheme of things, now seem to be on Satan's pay roll, helping to administer the reconditioning process) are able to dismiss the three exalted eavesdroppers and cut short one of Hell's most testing torments. The story seems to say that there may be mercy even in the abyss—that the lovers may in the end make something other than a hell for themselves, something other than a hell of Hell itself.

Debits and Credits begins with "The Enemies to Each Other," a retelling of the Adam and Eve story. In it the Divine Decree of Expulsion is worded, seemingly vindictively, "Get ye down, the one of you an enemy to the other." Yet, after the first couple have lost the power of laughter and become almost as the beasts, and after Adam, prompted by the Devil, has solemnly set up an altar to himself, and Eve has in due course followed suit, their enmity is seen to be a mitigation rather than an intensification of their exile. For, by exploiting it, the Archangel Jibrail enables them to regain the power of laughter, and to see themselves and each other for what they are. "By Allah I am no God but the mate of this most detestable Woman whom I love, and who is necessary to me beyond all the necessities," says Adam. And Eve, in her turn, replies: "By Allah I am no goddess in any sort, but the mate of this mere Man whom, in spite of all, I love beyond and above my soul."

Then said Adam: "O my Lady and Crown of my Torments, is it peace between us?" And our Lady Eve answered: "O my Lord and sole Cause of my Unreason, it is peace till the next time and the next occasion." And Adam said: "I accept, and I abide the chance." Our Lady Eve said: "O Man, wouldst thou have it otherwise upon any composition?" Adam said: "O Woman, upon no composition would I have it otherwise—not even for the return to the Garden of the Tree; and this I swear on thy head and the heads of all who shall proceed from thee." And Eve said: "I also." (31:22)

They then pull down the separate altars each has built, and on a new joint one they inscribe the words of the Decree of Expulsion, declaring it to be "both Our Curse and Our Blessing."

As in the Mowgli stories, man is not for Paradise, nor Paradise for man—either in the past or in the Archangel of the English's millennial future. Happiness and love are always, for Kipling, too dependent on, even too much a product of, their opposites. So Adam and Eve create a paradise out of their exile, as perhaps those other lovers do in Hell, and love out of their enmity. And laughter, as always, is the essential solvent when things reach an impasse.

Somewhat as he does in "The Children of the Zodiac," Kipling seems to use these two stories to sum up in more abstract and generalized form something of what he explores more freely in the best of the other stories from this period of his writing. They are, albeit tentatively, songs of having come through. Of his fables or parables for adults, those of this nature are much more interesting than those which merely express a preformed idea or ideology. Here he is as it were carrying the process of artistic creation, of bringing the chaotic material of raw experience under some sort of control and into some sort of order, a stage further. In a story like "The Bridge-Builders" we even see both stages of the process within the same piece of work.

It is probably fair to say that this desire to control and make sense of the formlessness of life, to reduce it to a kind of fictional diagram, is something which Kipling tends to carry to excess even in his naturalistic fiction. (Too much Apis, too little Chisto? At all events, an imbalance.) Certainly it is on stories such as "Black Jack" and "Without Benefit of Clergy" and "The Eye of Allah" and "The Wish House," rather than on "The Enemies to Each Other" or even "The Children of the Zodiac," that Kipling's reputation as a writer of fiction must rest. Nevertheless, accepting him (as any good wife must) for what he is rather than for what we would like to make of him, we may come to value even some of what we perceive to be his weaknesses as an integral part of what he uniquely has to offer. And stories of this more abstract kind, as an essential part of the means by which he came to terms with life, are also a part of what his art has to say to us.

Chapter Six
The Poetry

At the end of the previous chapter it was suggested that many of Kipling's stories have a tendency to be overly didactic—to serve too overtly as the vehicle for Kipling's own outlook on life. What is merely a tendency in his prose, however, becomes the dominant characteristic of his poetry. Those poems by which he is best remembered, such as "If" and "Recessional," are poems primarily of content, treasured by his admirers for their portable, versified wisdom. Among others, indeed, "Recessional," "The White Man's Burden" (dedicated to Theodore Roosevelt on the occasion of America's acquiring Cuba and the Philippines), and "The Islanders" (a swingeing attack on British complacency after the Boer War) were first published in *The Times*, and clearly regarded by Kipling as a form of journalism. Thus, whereas his prose often works indirectly, through allegory or symbol, his poetry relies in large measure on direct statement. It is not too much to say that his prose is often the more poetic and his poetry the more prosaic of these two media. For many readers, therefore, his collected poetical works are prudently and accurately entitled *The Definitive Edition of Rudyard Kipling's Verse*.

Not that everything he wrote in verse is a direct voicing of his own views, of course. His *Barrack Room Ballads*, for instance, are dramatic and/or narrative pieces, many of them written in dialect form. Yet, though the justly famous "Danny Deever" and the widely performed "Mandalay" are genuinely and engagingly dramatic, poems such as "Tommy," "Fuzzy-Wuzzy," "Screw Guns," and even "Gunga Din" are dramatic guises for all too familiar Kipling postures. And narratives such as "The Ballad of East and West" exemplify, in much cruder form than most of his prose stories, those imperial virtues of which, largely because of his poetry, he is so notorious an exponent.

Metrical Form

One not unexpected corollary of this downright, not to say dogmatic quality to so much of Kipling's verse is a downright or dogmatic quality to his rhythms. Not that they lack variety. Indeed, one reason for the unremitting beat to his work is that so much of what he wrote is in measures other than the iambic pentameter. This, as the most widely used meter in English poetry, is also the most flexible—the one with which poets have felt free to take those liberties which only familiarity sanctions. And the equal familiarity of the reader enables him to sustain a subliminal sense of those ten alternately stressed syllables through all a poet's departures from and variations upon that established metrical norm. Thus whereas in his iambic verse Longfellow is about average for his time in his use of reversed feet and extrametrical syllables, he employs virtually none of either in *Hiawatha*. The norm was not secure enough—was itself too much a departure from the norm—to allow of such cavalier treatment. And in a similar way Kipling's meters are both strong and unsubtle.

Unsubtle in this context does not, of course, mean unvaryingly monotonous. On the contrary, Kipling is both versatile and assured in his use of variation. In a poem like "The Ballad of East and West," for instance, he claims the right that Browning and Swinburne did before him to vary the number of syllables by substituting anapests for iambs at will. Reversed feet are much rarer, however, and never do we lose the sense, as we do in Swinburne, of whether the meter is basically a rising or falling one. Similarly, Kipling is almost addicted to the long line, prob-ably to give the appearance of having escaped from the rigidity of the balladlike meters of Scott and Macaulay. Yet almost invaria-bly such lines break in two at a consistently located caesura, often marked by a repetitive irregularity in the meter (usually a missing syllable), sometimes even by internal rhyme. In the same way, Kipling is very sparing in his use of enjambment, and quite insistent in his use of rhyme. The basic linear structure of his verse is something he is hesitant to tamper with.

Even when he does use an imabic pentameter, Kipling tends to be heavy-handedly end-stopped and repetitively regular.

> You couldn't pack a Broadwood half a mile—
> You mustn't leave a fiddle in the damp—
> You couldn't raft an organ up the Nile,
> And play it in an Equatorial swamp.[1]

Those lines are, perhaps unfairly, taken from "The Song of the Banjo." Songs are supposed to be end-stopped. In addition, moreover, the conventional kind of music to which we sing such songs ususally devotes a musical phrase or portion of the tune consisting of an even number of bars to each metrical line of the verse. Thus, if singing these words, we should be compelled to hold "mile" and "Nile" for three beats, and leave two beats rest after "damp" and "swamp." This characteristic is shown more clearly, perhaps, in these lines from "A Tale of Two Cities."

> Once, two hundred years age, the trader came
>   Meek and tame.
> Where his timid foot first halted, there he stayed,
>   Till mere trade
> Grew to Empire, and he sent his armies forth
>   South and North....

And here a further musical characteristic emerges in words which to my knowledge have never been set to music, but which read as so often in Kipling as though they ought to be sung. For the rhythm works better if we divide the words into four-syllable bars, and give major emphasis to the first stress within such a bar, and minor emphasis to the second. And it works best of all if we begin and end each line in the middle of such a bar.[2]

> Onče, twŏ / húndrĕd yeàrs ă / ġo, tñe tràdĕr / came   ˘
>   Meèk aǹd / táme.   ˘
> Whère hĭs / tîmĭd foòt fiřst / háltĕd, thère hĕ / stáyed,   ˘
>   Tîll mĕre / tráde.˙˙.

The next example, from "The Three-Decker," combines this pattern of four beats to the bar with the use of a beat's rest to mark at least every other caesura:

    Yoŭ'll / sée hĕr tièriñg / cánvăs   `   ˘ĭn /
          shéetĕd sìlvĕr / spŕead;   ˘   `
    Yoŭ'll / héar tñe loǹg-drăwn / thúndĕr 'nèath hĕr/
          léapiñg fiġuře- / héad;   ˘   `
    Whĭle / fár, sŏ fàr ă / bóve yŏu,   `   hĕr /
          táll pŏop-lànteřns / shĭne   ˘   `
    Uñ / véxed bÿ wìnd ŏr / wéathĕr ĺike tñe /
          cándlĕs roùnd ă / shŕine!   ˘   `

When the first foot of the line is trochaic, it seems that Kipling prefers to give it the lesser of the two stresses to a bar, but when it is iambic he awards it the major one. Illuminatingly, in *The Muse Among the Motors*, in which Horace, Chaucer, Milton, Longfellow, Emerson, and others write on various aspects of motoring, the concluding "Moral" (Author Unknown), in which Kipling clearly parodies himself, is written in just such a galumphing rhythm, changing midway from one to the other of the above variants.

Clearly there are limitations to any attempt to fit language into a precise musical (i.e., mathematical) framework, as all systems of scansion illustrate. Nevertheless, it is easier in Kipling's case than in that of most poets. This is true even in a poem like "Danny Deever," which employs, as T. S. Eliot rightly points out, a remarkable "combination of heavy beat and variation of pace."[3] For the heavy beat is still remarkably regular. The first foot of the poem is the only one to be reversed, and all nine of the extra syllables occur at the beginnings of lines, where they merely take up one of the two beats rest between the lines. Indeed, this set of Kipling's toward a musically regular rhythm is almost best illustrated where it is least insistent. In a poem such as "France," for instance, it is impossible to be at ease with what is clearly a more varied, supple rhythm than those of the examples above until one spots the consistently positioned metrical hiatus, sometimes but not always coincident with an obvious syntactic caesura.

> Ere our birth (rememberest thou?) side by side we lay
> Fretting in the womb of Rome to begin our fray.
> Ere men knew our tongues apart, our one task was known—
> Each to mould the other's fate as he wrought his own.

There are, of course, some felicitous irregularities in his less declamatory verse. "The Settler," for instance, makes a telling if fairly obvious use of anapests in the first, and of adjacent long stressed vowels in the fourth line of the following, to say nothing of apposite assonance in the second and skillfully alternating vowels in the third.

> Here, in the waves and the troughs of the plains,
>> Where the healing stillness lies,
> And the vast, benignant sky restrains
>> And the long days make wise—....

And in "Sussex" the transition from one line to another of "Belt upon belt, the wooded, dim, / Blue goodness of the Weald" combines a rare instance (despite the comma) of enjambment with the slowing down effect of three adjacent heavy syllables. We are propelled forcibly, yet at the same time deliberately, toward the emphatic richness of what might otherwise have been the rather trite vacuity of "goodness."

Yet such exceptions merely prove the rule that, for the most part, Kipling's rhythms are explicit rather than suggestive, declamatory rather than insinuating. And this is neither surprising nor inappropriate, since the poetry couched in such rhythms is, for the most part, a poetry of explicit and often declamatory statement.

Narrative and Dramatic Verse

There are, of course, exceptions to such a generalization. The masterly "Danny Deever," written so soon after Kipling's return to London and so early in his poetic career, has all the repetitive economy, all the apparent particularity and inherent universality of "Edward, Edward" and "Lord Randal." That the conversation between the sergeant and his squad is entirely unspoken only adds to its grim intensity, as do such touches of impatient humor as:

> "What makes the rear-rank breathe so 'ard?"
>   said Files-on-Parade.
> "It's bitter cold, it's bitter cold," the
>   Colour-Sergeant said.
> "What makes that front-rank man fall down?"
>   said Files-on-Parade.
> "A touch o' sun, a touch o' sun," the Colour-
>   Sergeant said.

The language is colloquial in Kipling's best manner, which means he does not overdo it. And the "poetry" is so sparse yet so precise that we feel no incongruity in hearing it from such authentic speakers.

> "What's that so black agin the sun?" said Files-
>   on-Parade.
> "It's Danny fightin' 'ard for life," the Colour-
>   Sergeant said.
> "What's that that whimpers over'ead?" said Files-
>   on-Parade.
> "It's Danny's soul that's passin' now," the Colour-
>   Sergeant said.

Even the length of the poem is just right: three stanzas plus varying refrains to define the occasion, set the scene, and establish the chief actor, and one for the climax. Best of all, there is no word of generalized comment or moralizing. The poem's strength in all these respects becomes clear if it is read alongside "The Widow's Party" (the Widow being Queen Victoria), a much more self-conscious imitation of "Edward, Edward" in form and style, and of "Lord Randal" in theme. The latter does a fair job of

making Kipling's point that the soldier's lot is not a happy one.
Yet, though its original readers may have nodded their heads in
sage approval, and admired Kipling's dexterity, there is no *fris-
son* of recognition as the reader's field of experience expands and
then comes full circle home again. The incident is a cardboard-
cutout allegory.

There are a few other remarkable successes in the ballad form
worth noting. "My Boy Jack" is a justly famous response to the
grief and pride of all parents bereaved by war, though ostensibly
about a mother whose son fought in the Battle of Jutland. More
eerily unnerving because arising out of or appropos no obvious
external stimulus is "The Gift of the Sea." A young woman, her
husband killed at sea, grieves with her mother over the dead body
of her child, when they hear a cry from the sea in the storm
outside. The grandmother argues it is the cry of the child's soul
unable to find its way, that it is a lamb, or sea birds, and tries to
comfort her daughter. Finally the daughter will not be pacified.

> She put her mother aside,
>   "In Mary's name let be!
> "For the peace of my soul I must go," she said,
>   And she went to the calling sea.
>
> In the heel of the wind-bit pier,
>   Where the twisted weed was piled,
> She came to the life she had missed by an hour,
>   For she came to a little child.
>
> She laid it unto her breast,
>   And back to her mother she came,
> But it would not feed and it would not heed,
>   Though she gave it her own child's name.
>
> And the dead child dripped on her breast,
>   And her own in the shroud lay stark;
> And "God forgive us, mother," she said,
>   "We let it die in the dark!"

The title would seem to have us view the poem as a kind of allegory, urging us not to ignore such consolations as life sends us. Yet the poem to me is about an unheard child rather than a bereaved mother. It is also, perhaps, the work of that post-Pre-Raphaelite, 1890s poet Kipling might have become if he had never returned to India.

Not all Kipling's narratives are so sorrowful or so mysterious, however. The famous "Ballad of East and West," despite the insistent rhythms of its long lines being uncomfortably reminiscent of Robert Service, deserves to stand within striking distance of Macaulay's "Horatio" and Tennyson's "The Revenge" as a heroic literary ballad of Victorian vintage. The genre is different from that of the old border ballads, mainly in being much more self-consciously "heroic," as befits work written for an age uneasily and increasingly aware of the unheroic springs of so many of its actions. The poem begins with that most often quoted line of Kipling's, "Oh, East is East and West is West, and never the twain shall meet," and then proceeds to demonstrate what those who make use of the quotation never seem to remember, that "there is neither East nor West, Border, nor Breed, nor Birth,/ When two strong men stand face to face, though they come from the ends of the earth!" Perhaps the ending is too pat. The Pathan chieftain who has stolen the colonel's horse and is pursued by the colonel's son, alone, so admires the young man's spirit that he sends his own son back with him to be trained as a soldier. So, though there is no East or West as long as the "two strong men stand face to face," acknowledging each other as equals, readers are reassured as to the long-term, inherent superiority of the West. Still, it is a good rousing yarn, with very little moralizing.

Already, you will note, the tone of the comment has become mildly condescending. We cannot long keep up the pretense that Kipling is as other poets are. Nevertheless, we must first consider a few more masterpieces which, though very clearly the work of Kipling, need no apology before we may think of them as poems. Two remarkable dramatic monologues certainly demand our attention—"McAndrew's Hymn" and "The Mary Gloster."

Both are written in typically long, strongly rhythmic Kipling lines, though with the flexibility that befits a dramatic rather than a narrative form. McAndrew quickly establishes himself as a typical Scottish ship's engineer as seen by Kipling—"Predestination in the stride o' yon connectin'-rod." Yet he is by no means a caricature. Indeed, the poem is chiefly memorable for expressing, in verse, Kipling's enthusiasm for machines and all who tend them. No one has more successfully captured the romance of the machine than he does here.

Lord, send a man like Robbie Burns to sing the Song o' Steam!
To match wi' Scotia's noblest speech yon orchestra sublime
Whaurto—uplifted like the Just—the tail-rods mark the time.
The crank-throws give the double-bass, the feed-pump sobs an' heaves,
An' now the main eccentrics start their quarrel on the sheaves:
Her time, her own appointed time, the rocking link-head bides,
Till—hear that note?—the rod's return whings glimmerin' through the
          guides.
They're all awa'! True beat, full power, the clangin' chorus goes
Clear to the tunnel where they sit, my purrin' dynamoes.
Interdependence absolute, foreseen, ordained, decreed,
To work, Ye'll note, at ony tilt an' every rate o' speed.
Fra' skylight-lift to furnace-bars, backed, bolted, braced an' stayed,
An' singin' like the Mornin' Stars for joy that they are made;
While, out o' touch o' vanity, the sweatin' thrust-block says:
"Not unto us the praise, or man—not unto us the praise!"
Now, a' together, hear them lift their lesson—theirs an' mine:
"Law, Orrder, Duty an' Restraint, Obedience, Discipline!"

The climax of the passage also expresses "the utter Doctrine itself" according to Kipling, but transposed to the world of the engineer.

McAndrew's is the sad if triumphant story of a man who has watched others feather their nests in ways he has had neither the time nor the inclination to pursue or stoop to. "The Mary Gloster" is a success story, but equally sad. In a way which irresistably recalls the Bishop ordering his tomb, Sir Anthony Gloster, master of a fleet of ships, tries to explain to his bored, incompetent son how to circumvent the board and shareholders in order to carry out his father's carefully planned whim to be buried at sea and lie, "ten thousand miles away," beside his wife. In contrast to McAndrew's life, Sir Anthony's has been one of risks and far-reaching decisions taken with the one end of success in view. He is, therefore, a less immediately sympathetic character. To counterbalance this, the situation presented in the poem is far more dramatic and calculated to win our sympathy. Both poems are worthy tributes to the Browning Kipling admired, "McAndrew's Hymn" being more clearly what Kipling alone could have written.

A poem it could only have occurred to Kipling to write, "Sestina of the Tramp-Royal" is a dramatic monologue in dialect and, as the title implies, sestina form. It is easily the most successful of Kipling's wanderlust poems, probably because of the restraint exercised by the form on a theme which all too easily in poems of this period, whether by Kipling or Masefield or Gerald Gould, leads to an excess of nostalgia for what has never been. Another dramatic lyric on a similar theme which is worth noting is "For to Admire." There are more false touches than in the "Sestina," yet Kipling weds his music-hall dialect form to a lyrical voicing of emotion with unexpected success. More uniformly assured of its touch, the beautiful "Lichtenberg" lets an Australian soldier in South Africa tell us how the smell of wattle stirs up memories of home.

> And I saw Sydney the same as ever,
>   The picnics and brass-bands;
> And my little homestead on Hunter River
>   And my new vines joining hands.
> It all came over me in one act
>   Quick as a shot through the brain—
> With the smell of the wattle round Lichtenberg,
>   Riding in, in the rain.

Only a man as rootless as Kipling could use another man's homesickness, for a continent he himself had scarcely set foot on, to express his longing for somewhere to be homesick about. This, in fact, he was already in the process of finding, in Sussex. And in the poem of that name, as in *Puck of Pook's Hill* and *Rewards and Fairies*, an integral part of the landscape was a sense of its history—something that, for all their attractions, was missing in the landscapes of America, Africa, and Australia.

> Clean of officious fence or hedge,
>   Half-wild and wholly tame,
> The wise turf cloaks the white cliff-edge
>   As when the Romans came.
> What sign of those that fought and died
>   At shift of sword and sword?
> The barrow and the camp abide,
>   The sunlight and the sward

With "Sussex," however, we have reached the poetry of direct authorial statement, the poetry that comprises by far the greater part of Kipling's output, and in which lie the difficulties we can no longer postpone facing. For Kipling in most of what he wrote is no Wallace Stevens, nor even a Robert Frost, no T. S. Eliot or W. H. Auden, even though there is a didacticism and a metrical versatility to Auden and a country wisdom to Frost which recall certain aspects of his output. There is in their work a complex subtlety of emotional response, and a supple strength of intellectual response to that response, which is lacking in Kipling's. Telltale "spots of commonness" show through even in Kipling's prose, and for some readers disqualify if from serious consideration alongside that of, say, Conrad or Lawrence. But how much more so in his poetry! That ever-present temptation, as we have noted, to be the knowing commentator on the action in his stories is often the sole *raison d'être* and constituent of his poetry. Very seldom is the event or image itself allowed to make the point. In many cases there is no event or dramatic speaker—sometimes not even a single image. Moreover, even in poems like "Lichtenberg" or "Sestina of the Tramp-Royal" or "Sussex," the emotions are essentially commonplace, such as any reader is capable not only of feeling but of self-dramatizing quite adequately. They may be more memorably expressed than anything the reader would be capable of writing, but they are unilluminated at some more profound or transcendent level.

Didactic Verse

At this point perhaps we should remind ourselves of Pope's paraphrase of the above—"What oft was thought [or felt] but ne'er so well express'd." For, with the exception of Shakespeare (55 pp.), Tennyson (14 pp.), and Milton (13 pp.), and well ahead of Pope (6 pp.), Kipling (10 pp.) has more space devoted to him than anyone else in the 1941 edition of the *Oxford Dictionary of Quotations*. Nine of those pages, moreover, are from his poetry. He is, of course, eminently quotable. The lines cited include "Oh, East is East and West is West, and never the twain shall meet"; "And a woman is only a woman, but a good cigar is a smoke"; "Teach us delight in simple things,/And mirth that hath no bitter springs,/Forgiveness free of evil done,/And love to all men neath the sun!"; "But the backbone of the Army is the Non-commissioned man"; "And what should they know of England who only England know?"; "The female of the species is more deadly than the male"; "You're a better man than I am, Gunga Din!"; "If you can keep your head when all around you..../ And—which is more—you'll be a man, my son!"; "For the Colonel's Lady and Judy O'Grady/Are sisters under the skin"; "Ship me somewhere East of Suez, where the best is like the worst,/Where there aren't no Ten Commandments, an' a man can raise a thirst"; "And the end of the fight is a tombstone white with the name of the late deceased,/And the epitaph drear: 'A Fool lies here who tried to hustle the East' "; " ... lesser breeds without the law"; "Take up the White Man's Burden."

Condescendingly racist, condescendingly sexist, resoundingly commonplace, and flattering on all such counts to a like-minded readership—yes, the charges are probably true, and go far toward explaining Kipling's popularity. Or, to express it another way, those critics are probably right who see the two most powerful influences on Kipling's poetry as being the music hall and *Hymns*

Ancient and Modern. But the influence was probably not exclusively metrical, as is usually argued; he may well have drawn just as much by way of content and style from these two repositories of the two sides to the average mind, just as he has since contributed to both.

He was, as no other comparable literary figure has ever been, the people's poet. By using such a term, however, I am not implying anything about the social class of his admirers. These included brigadiers and rear admirals and members of Parliament and bishops even more than barmaids and taxi-drivers and private soldiers, though he reached them, too. No, by "people" I mean those for whom, in spite of all the efforts of enlightened teachers, a poem still has rhyme, meter, and a message. And Kipling, in a high proportion of his verse, is using rhyme and meter to enhance the forceful expression of those insights and prejudices which he considered worldly wisdom—not necessarily wisdom for all time, but at least for his lifetime and those of his children.

Sometimes the views he expresses are such that present-day readers will find them repugnant. "Ulster" was for too long a favorite in Northern Ireland classrooms for Kipling not to bear some small responsibility for the present impasse. And "The Stranger," labeled a Canadian poem in the *Definitive Edition*, articulates just too faithfully and flatteringly the stubborn sources of racial intolerance for Canadians at this juncture of their country's history to thank him. But perhaps the poem which, somewhat unjustly, has aroused most thoroughly the ire of subsequent generations of liberals is the one which was most applauded on its appearance.

> God of our fathers, known of old,
>   Lord of our far-flung battle-line,
> Beneath whose awful Hand we hold
>   Dominion over palm and pine—
> Lord God of Hosts, be with us yet,
>   Lest we forget—lest we forget!

The tumult and the shouting dies;
    The Captains and the Kings depart:
Still stands Thine ancient sacrifice,
    An humble and a contrite heart.
Lord God of Hosts, be with us yet,
Lest we forget—lest we forget!

Far-called, our navies melt away;
    On dune and headland sinks the fire:
Lo, all our pomp of yesterday
    Is one with Nineveh and Tyre!
Judge of the Nations, spare us yet,
Lest we forget—lest we forget!

If, drunk with sight of power, we loose
    Wild tongues that have not Thee in awe,
Such boastings as the Gentiles use,
    Or lesser breeds without the Law—
Lord God of Hosts, be with us yet,
Lest we forget—lest we forget!

For heathen heart that puts her trust
    In reeking tube and iron shard,
All valiant dust that builds on dust,
    And guarding, calls not Thee to guard,
For frantic boast and foolish word—
Thy mercy on Thy People, Lord!

"Recessional" was actually intended, among all the euphoria
surrounding Queen Victoria's Diamond Jubilee, to be a solemn
warning against imperial pride. But its quiet assumption that the
British are "Thy People" and all the rest "Gentiles," and that
consequently Britain's "Dominion over palm and pine" is
divinely sanctioned, together with the incongruous juxtaposition
of its admonition to "An humble and contrite heart" and its
unctuous air of superiority in the fourth stanza, has alternately
enraged and amused antiimperialists ever since. It is, of course,
possible to defend certain misunderstood details. The "lesser

breeds without the Law" are not, as is usually assumed when the phrase is quoted out of context, Asians and Africans, but Germans (if that makes things any better). Their less well bred, more openly arrogant imperialism was already alarming Kipling in 1897. Similarly, the "heathen heart" for which Kipling asks forgiveness in the last stanza is clearly not a Hindu or Moslem heart (they were far from "heathen" in Kipling's view), but a heathen British heart which forgets. More importantly and positively, the poem possesses a prophetic power and authority which must give even its present-day readers pause, however fleetingly. Yet, when all is said, the lines must be read as addressed to a nation serene in its belief that, for the foreseeable future, the sun would continue not to set on the greatest empire of all time, and that, in the main, this was for the good of all concerned. Such a mood is, of course, totally irrecapturable.

This, from a strictly literary point of view, is almost a pity. For the poem is a fine piece of restrained rhetoric. The opening stanza is largely attributive for its first five lines, even the "far-flung battle-line" and "Dominion over palm and pine" contributing syntactically to the sustained and periodic greater glory of God. Only in the anticlimactic last line does man hold center stage. But this he continues to do in the self-contained first two lines of the second stanza, whose so quotable alliterative balance is in static and marked contrast to the syntax of the first stanza. And the third stanza continues to use the self-contained single line or pair of lines to itemize the transience of man. Then, to give mounting urgency to the poem's repeated behests for humility, the fourth and fifth stanzas revert to a periodic structure. The fourth loses momentum somewhat in its appositively explanatory third and fourth lines, but the final stanza, by dropping the refrain of "Lest we forget," maintains its periodic build-up right to the last line.

Perhaps a minor work of art like this, seeming to speak only to its own time and place and having little to say to the world we live in, could be valued merely as a period piece. Perhaps we should regard it more as we do good antique furniture or a good second-rate portrait. Such a notion might save more than the poems of Kipling from failing to meet overly high expectations. Maybe we should commission someone to record, equally faithfully and sincerely, our own equally serene assumption that Western economic and technological paternalism is for the good of all whose third-world lives it touches. Readers in the future will probably enjoy an occasional boost to their self-esteem, just as we do those that Kipling affords.

Or might it help them to perceive their own paternalisms, as Kipling—or Defoe, for that matter, in *Robinson Crusoe*—may help us to perceive ours? The old truism has it that the major artist transcends his age whereas the minor one transmits it. And in doing so, complete with its blind spots, he may enable readers in future ages to deduce the likelihood of similar blind spots in their own. All of which does nothing to rescue Kipling, at least as poet, from the status of a minor writer. But it may help put him in company not entirely to be despised.

The equally famous or notorious "If" has fared both better and worse than "Recessional." On the one hand, as a compendium of moral maxims, it may well still be being discovered by new readers as a kind of secular decalogue. Yet on the other, just because it is more likely still to be taken seriously, others will find its reduction of a minefield of moral complexities to a series of simplistic equations, and its advocacy in the final stanza of a kind of emotional cocoon, where neither friend nor foe can really reach you, dangerous. Probably the best way to read the poem today, though at an appropriately less exalted level, is much as we read *An Essay on Man*. (The paragraph beginning "Know then thyself, presume not God to scan" is even more rigorously, if also more deftly and exquisitely, mathematical than "If.") This way we can admire its workmanlike handling of the subject matter, recognize the worth of some of its insights, but value it chiefly as another period piece—as a nostalgic sampler, in fact, from an age when a combination of willpower and firm moral direction could be seen as the solution. Whether it was the solution is another matter; whether anything is is always another matter.

"Songs from Books"

I am, of coure, implying a marked contrast between Kipling's largely two-dimensional verse, and the more subtle and varied perspectives to be found in the best of his prose, where the complexities of the human situation are shown as timelessly recurrent, under whatever difference of guise. This will emerge most clearly from a parallel examination of some of the poems Kipling attaches to most of his later stories, and of the stories themselves. If one were to speculate in the abstract about the likely function of such poems, he would see it, surely, as to open a further door—to suggest, by means readily available to poetry, some layer of mystery or meaning the story had not been able to handle. Yet too often Kipling's poems merely make explicit, repeat in simplified and more didactic form, or even falsify, what is quite sufficiently implicit in the story. "If," for instance, is printed as an envoi or epilogue to "Brother Square Toes," and is clearly intended to comment on the difficult tightrope Washington was having to walk in avoiding a further war with Britain. Yet the poem, despite the literal meaning of its words, undercuts by the neatness with which very real dilemmas are epigrammatized, and by the ease with which it arrives at its triumphant conclusion, the implications of the story. For, in the two glimpses we are given of him, we sense above all the difficulty Washington was experiencing in maintaining his strict self-control.

In the case of "The Beginning," appended to "Mary Postgate," the poem falsifies the effect of the story even more seriously. Almost as if it had been written beforehand about the story Kipling thought he was going to write, it proudly warns the Germans of the consequences of having taught the English, at long last, to hate. But the story itself, as we have seen, leaves us aghast at war's effect on Mary Postgate. In "Song of the Men's Side" Kipling merely retells the story somewhat less effectively, in verse form, of "The Knife and the Naked Chalk." "Neighbours," which precedes "Beauty Spots," does no more than rather heavy-handedly point the moral that neighbors should be good neighbors. And "The Expert," which follows the same story, almost equally clumsily underlines an irony that should and could have been implicit in the story. Finally, as its title implies, "Untimely" anticipates in general terms the theme which "The Eye of Allah" then goes on to exemplify in such a dramatic and individualized manner. In all the above cases, and many others, the poems are patently less poetic than the stories, and express in an overt, discursive, essentially prosaic manner what is implied, or could easily have been implied, in the story itself.

It should be said, in fairness, that "The Last Ode," the poem following "The Eye of Allah," is a translation or adaptation of Horace (5:31) which superbly, suggestively, takes up where the story leaves off and leads us, tentatively, forward. It should also be admitted that "The Looking Glass" ("Gloriana") deepens our understanding of the story by showing us the narrator in a way she herself could not have done, and that "The Way through the Woods" ("Marklake Witches") irradiates not so much the story it is attached to as the frame, and thereby the whole interrelationship of past and present explored in *Rewards and Fairies*, besides being a poem justly famous in its own right. It should finally be acknowledged that in "Butterflies" ("Wireless") Kipling uses an allegory or analogy to indicate how he wishes us to regard the paranormal element in the story. This last is worth examining in detail.

> Eyes aloft, over dangerous places,
> The children follow the butterflies
> And, in the sweat of their upturned faces,
> Slash with a net at the empty skies.
>
> So it goes they fall amid brambles,
> And sting their toes on the nettle-tops,
> Till, after a thousand scratches and scrambles,
> They wipe their brows and the hunting stops.
>
> Then to quiet them comes their father
> And stills the riot of pain and grief,
> Saying, "Little ones, go and gather
> Out of my garden a cabbage-leaf."

> "You will find on it whorls and clots of
> Dull grey eggs that, properly fed,
> Turn, by way of worms, to lots of
> Glorious butterflies, raised from the dead."...

> "Heaven is beautiful, Earth is ugly,"
> The three-dimensioned preacher saith;
> So we must not look where the snail and the slug lie
> For Psyche's birth.... And that is our death!

Children/humans chase butterflies/beauty/mystery in the sky, fruitlessly. Their father (God? So detailed an allegory seems unlikely under "empty skies") shows them that beauty/mystery, which conventional religious attitudes regard as the prerogative of heaven, have earthly origins. Kipling's use of "three-dimensioned" is particularly interesting. By it he implies, presumably, the orthodox tripartite spiritual cosmos of Heaven, Earth, and Hell, with more things on earth than are dreamt of in the preacher's philosophy as the fourth dimension.

This is a genuine use of poetic form to extend and expand the meaning of the preceding story. Most importantly, it takes us beyond the mystifyingly occult events of the story as told, toward the far deeper mystery of how any artist comes by his inspiration, and in particular how an averagely ill-educated tubercular apothecary came to write "The Eve of Saint Agnes." Yet "Butterflies" itself was clearly not the product of any such mysterious process, but a controlled, calculated attempt—as allegory always is, in contrast to metaphor or symbol—to give oblique expression to a predetermined meaning. Kipling is in fact using allegory here as it has been suggested he uses parable in "Uncovenanted Mercies," "The Enemies to Each Other" and "The Children of the Zodiac." Once again we find this doubt in Kipling's mind as to whether narrative, however carefully crafted and strewn with clues, has made his meaning clear. Once again, despite all the dangers of oversimplification, he supplements narrative with abstract didacticism.

Kipling seems almost never to explore a form or image or
cadence for its own sake, with the idea of discovering what it is he
wants to say. Instead, he knows what he wants to say, and uses,
indeed chooses, form and image and cadence in order to say it.
Obviously it is possible to write a poem which takes a story as its
starting point and then finds its own way onward and outward.
Sometimes this is what Kipling does. But much more often it
seems as if he has not yet found a way of using words to pin down
quite securely enough the booty brought back by his latest "raid
on the inarticulate." The expression he gives it in the story may
suffice, may indeed be the most satisfactory form he arrives at.
But, just in case, he uses verse to clinch matters, *because verse for
Kipling is a definitive rather than an exploratory, open-ended
medium*. Thus Eliot can say, in some puzzlement, "Kipling does
write poetry, but that is not what he is setting out to do." And
later, "I know of no writer of such great gifts for whom poetry
seems to have been more purely an instrument." Yet, as he also
admits, "there is hardly any poem, even in the collected works, in
which he fails to do what he has set out to do."[4]
We are talking here of verse and/or poetry which is so different in nature and intent, and in the presuppositions of its author,
from other nineteenth- and twentieth-century poetry that it is
difficult to conceive of its having been written, or read, as literature. Eliot would have us see Kipling as a balladeer, writing what
must convey its story (or message) to its listeners at one hearing.
To me Kipling seems too much the conscious craftsman for this
to be a sufficient account of what he is doing. Tentatively, I would
suggest a parallel with the neoclassical period. Then it was not
regarded as inherently unpoetic to give poetic form to public
attitudes and the concerns of polity rather than the everlasting
preoccupations of the self. Then at least it was no shameful
admission to speak of poetic form as that which (as Coleridge
complains) added embellishments and gave elegance and mem-
orability to something which could have existed in prose form.
Indeed, as the poet's intention, it had existed in a protoprose
form, before pen was even set to paper. This is not to deny that

the act of poetic creation often added what the poet was not aware of intending, whether in Pope's case or Kipling's. But I question whether we are justified in attempting too strenuously to confer honorary modernity on either the Augustans or on that poor man's Dryden, Kipling, by regarding such unconscious elements in their verse as their sole or major claim to poetic status.

Kipling, then, wrote a number of fine pieces of verse, mostly narrative or dramatic, which no one would deny are poems. He also wrote a great deal of topical, occasional, and light verse which is just that. Sometimes, in such work, there will be an image, a line of rare simplicity, a flash of true poetry. And he wrote some fine polemic verses whose rhetorical craft and strength of feeling would, in an age more sympathetic to such writing, entitle them to the status of poetry, but which many may find it difficult to acknowledge as such in today's climate of taste. In most of what he wrote, content was paramount, and the poetry a means to an end. This fact in itself is source enough of offense to many. Add to it that the outdated and often distasteful views he held on matters of the day are so much more openly stated in his verse than in his prose, so much more naked and unqualified, and it seems unlikely his verse will ever regain the measure of esteem his prose has begun to receive.

Chapter Seven
Kipling and Conrad: Conclusion

Probably the main obstacle to be overcome in trying to sum up Kipling is the sheer range and diversity of his work, as well as the wide readership to which he appeals. There is, in the first place, the fact that he appears as ambidextrously at home in verse as in prose. We may clearly value his prose more than his verse, and there is some internal evidence that Kipling himself came to do so. Yet all his life he continued to write both with equal freedom, and to link them to an increasing extent, deliberately using the one to complement or act as a foil to the other. Confusingly, however, he often seems to have employed verse in a more essentially prosaic manner than he did prose.

Turning to the subject matter of his stories, we find a bewildering variety. There are tales set in India, America, Africa, Germany, France, England, and on the high seas, as well as in prehistoric, Roman, medieval, and Renaissance times, to say nothing of the eighteenth, nineteenth, twentieth, and twenty-first centuries. There are accounts of battles, of supernatural encounters, and of the inner spiritual struggles of holy men; there are descriptions of the varying skills of bridge-builders, ships' engineers, soldiers, journalists, administrators, doctors, priests, and artists; there are stories whose protagonists range from commanding officers to private soldiers, from cabinet ministers and the Chairman of A.B.C. to cook-housekeepers and farm laborers, not to mention children, animals, locomotives, the parts of a ship and the very winds and waves. The mere fact that Kipling remained so faithful to the short story rather than the novel, moreover, is evidence of his need just as much as his aptitude for such a form, as one permitting him this kind of range and variety.

149

As for the styles and approaches Kipling uses, here too all seems to be variety. In the greater part of what he writes he clearly relies on realism, both of incident and speech. Yet in an unusually high proportion of his stories he is equally clearly addicted to fable, parable, and allegory. As in the case of his prose and verse, moreover, the former is more often open-ended and suggestive, the latter more precise and didactic. In the Pyecroft and Mulvaney stories above all, but over and over again elsewhere also, Kipling patently feels a need for the release of tension supplied by comedy. Yet in "Without Benefit of Clergy" and "The Wish House" he comes as close to tragedy as is possible in twenty-five pages or so, and achieves varying degrees of pathos in many other stories. In his prose style he can be as stark and direct as in "The Story of Muhammad Din"and " Little Tobrah,"as archaically embellished as in "The Enemies to Each Other," as richly tapestried as in "The Eye of Allah," or as flamboyant and idiosyncratic as in the speaking voices of Mulvaney and Pyecroft. And in his mode of narration he can be as economic as in "Beyond the Pale," "My Sunday at Home," and "The Gardener," as convoluted as in "The Bonds of Discipline," as enigmatic as in "Mrs. Bathurst," or as dramatically ironic as in "Marklake Witches" and "A Doctor of Medicine."

There is even variety in Kipling's frequent use of a narrator. Within such variety, however, there is a polarizing dichotomy which, paradoxically, may help us find the overall pattern or unity amid the diversity. Sometimes, as in the case of "A Sahibs' War," the narration is a pure dramatic monologue with an implied listener. Elsewhere, as in most of *Plain Tales from the Hills*, we are told the tale by a fairly opinionated "I" narrator who presumably witnessed or was himself told about the events he describes, but who played no part in them. Most often, one (or more) of the characters relates certain events in which he (or they) played a major or minor role. One of the listeners is a secondary narrator or scribe, and he in turn transmits the whole, frame and yarn alike, to the reader, much as the narrator-scribe records Conrad's Marlow stories for us. One function of such a format is to provide continuity between groups of stories with the same distinctive narrator. Another, as in "Black Jack," and "The Man Who Would Be King," is to provide the narrative with a frame which in some way sets it off. But in most cases this technique owes most to Kipling's love affair with the spoken word.

It has often been remarked that Kipling conveys the sensuous ambience of the events he describes with peculiar vividness. And of nothing is this more true than the speaking voices of his characters. Indeed, speech is Kipling's principal method of characterization. One thinks of the clipped, throw-away self-deprecation of all those subalterns, the bureaucratese of the Archangel of the English, the self-indulgence of grown men reverting to being schoolboys in "Slaves of the Lamp," or the color and pungency of Mahbub Ali's speech in *Kim*, by contrast with the way Huree Babu interlaces his way of saying things with incongruous idioms picked up from his English contacts. And where a single narrator tells all or most of a story, whether "A Conference of the Powers," "Dray Wara Yow Dee," or "On Greenhow Hill," he lends character to the whole narrative. The overall effect of this is to create still more variety, since Kipling's ear was attuned to a wide range of voices and accents, and he clearly enjoyed exercising his virtuoso skill at reproducing them on paper. Louis Cornell, writing of the gift Kipling showed even in his schoolboy verse for imitation and parody, states:

A skilful parodist at eighteen, Kipling never lost his ability to imitate the mannerisms of other authors, but he never fully developed the gift of assimilation: unlike Joyce and Eliot and Pound, he never learned to use the work of earlier writers in such a way as to make it his own.[1]

And what is true of the writers Kipling imitates is equally true of the speakers whose intonations he captures. For instance, apart from indicating that their common author enjoyed reproducing the spoken word and had a certain talent for it, the conversations recorded in the three sea stories, *Captains Courageous*, "Their

Lawful Occasions," and "The Manner of Men," give us little sense of the essential Kipling quality they share. Each new set of cadences, and therefore each new story, seems a fresh start.

On the other hand, there are those other narrators, or narrator-scribes, all of them to a greater or lesser extent Kipling in disguise. Admittedly, it has been argued that the "I" of *Plain Tales from the Hills* is not to be identified with Kipling. Yet unless the two could often be mistaken for one another, any ironic distancing Kipling achieves would lose its subtlety and point. And clearly it is the same commentator ubiquitously pontificating in all the stories and lending a quasi-didactic unity to the whole collection. Similarly, the recurring Kipling-like narrator of the late Masonic stories links them by means of a shared set of values and a common tone. And much the same can be said of those stories ("Slaves of the Lamp," "The Honours of War," "A Deal in Cotton") where veterans of USC and/or India forgather and Beetle narrates.

Thus the presence of a narrator in such a high proportion of Kipling's stories serves two seemingly opposed ends. Used in one way, it ensures a wide range of narrative tone, and adds to the overall variety of his work. Used in another, it allows him to impose a recurring and often somewhat didactic tone, not far removed from his own. Kipling yearns equally, it seems, for the negative capability of the chameleon and the pulpit privileges of the egotistical sublime. Such a duality is at least reminiscent, moreover, of those already noted between his realistic fiction and his parables or fables, between his prose and his verse, between his spare and his embellished prose styles, and between his controlled and his free-wheeling modes of narration. Yet a balance or bargain between such opposing tendencies is merely that which must always be struck, in each and every creative act, between the chaotic richness of life and the exigencies of artistic form. All that is unusual, in Kipling's case, is that the contrast between these two sides to his head seems particularly acute. Few authors can rival the immediacy with which he creates the whole diverse world of the five senses—indeed, a whole series of such worlds. Yet few are more committed than Kipling to using their writing to point the moral, underline the message, spread the gospel.

The gospel of what? Above all, clearly, that of law and order, of discipline, of hard work, of respect for skill and know-how and efficiency, of the wisdom of experience rather than mere book learning. Yet, in a dichotomy of content paralleling those of style noted above, this emphasis on a highly controlled quality to life must be set against Kipling's love of laughter and of almost anarchical farce. The wisdom of age, moreover, is so often to be found in alliance with the enthusiasm and the vitality of youth, whether in the persons of Baloo and Mowgli, the Lama and Kim, Sergius and Valens, or the commanding officers and subalterns who populate such stories as "The Tomb of His Ancestors" and "Only a Subaltern." Most insistently of all, as we have noted of "On the City Wall," "Without Benefit of Clergy," "The Bridge-Builders," and above all of *Kim*, the need for law and order as represented by the British is counterbalanced by the Lalun-like attractions of India's corrupt and chaotic variety. The same antagonism is apparent, moreover, between the forces contending for the soul of Mulvaney, with neither Kipling nor his readers wanting to see absolute victory for either side.

Many people's hostility to Kipling is the result, one suspects, of their not sensing his saving ambivalences, and taking him at his word when he is sounding off about law and order and the faults of democracy. As already noted more than once, Kipling the artist is far wiser than this, and knows that complete victory for the forces of law and order would be as disastrous as the triumph of chaos. He acknowledges as much, clearly if almost sadly, in "As Easy as A.B.C." Some sort of precarious equilibrium, as achieved at the end of *Kim*, and as advocated so far as the artist is concerned in "The Bull that Thought," is the best man can hope for.

Kipling is not an easy author to place among his contemporaries, but a brief comparison with E. M. Forster and Joseph Conrad, one somewhat younger, the other a little older than he was, may help us to see him in a clearer perspective.

At first sight Kipling and Forster have nothing in common other than their differences on the subject of India. Yet Forster's constant quest is best summarized in the epigraph to *Howards End*: "Only Connect." And in *A Passage to India*, despite his satire of the Sahibs, and more particularly of the Memsahibs, he explores and attempts to bridge the chasm that yawns between the races. What it is about Indians that infuriates the British is exposed just as clearly as what it is that Indians cannot stand about the British. Furthermore, the underlying causes of such cultural differences are examined—in particular, the nature of Hinduism, with its emphasis on passive acceptance rather than active attempts to change things. The two characters to whom Forster entrusts his bridge-building, however, are both to some extent disconnected outsiders and onlookers. Fielding, the college principal, is regarded as less and less "pukka" by his fellow countrymen as the story proceeds, and Aziz, whom Forster chooses to make a Moslem, is ultimately as baffled as Fielding or Forster by the Hindu mind. Perhaps Forster's boldest attempt to come to grips with Hinduism is to present Professor Godbole, the Brahmin, as an essentially comic character. This underlines Hinduism's willingness to incorporate even the comic and the ridiculous within its all-encompassing world view. Yet within the book it serves further to distance the professor from the rational tone of both Fielding and Forster. And the use of a wasp to connect those two mystics of East and West, Godbole and Mrs. Moore, is almost a gesture of despair at the impossibility of the task. The book is too honest to do other than let us understand more clearly why it is impossible, as yet, to connect.

Yet Kipling, as we have seen, does connect. He is not, as Forster is, the self-sufficient, disinterested onlooker, attempting to interpret the rest of us to each other. The connections he works out are connections within his own polarized self. Forster attempts to transmit to his readers a deeper understanding of Hinduism than they are in all likelihood capable of grasping in the first place, and fails—though we must salute the failure. Kipling, on the other hand, attempts to capture as much of the Lama's philosophy as is already intuitively a part of his own makeup (though a small part, perhaps), and to reconcile it with all the other seeming irreconcilables of which he is composed. And he makes his connections, builds his bridges, not so much through rational explanation or analysis as by an unconscious balancing of opposing tendencies within the very texture of his writing. Kipling may not introspect, or have his characters do so, with any great success. But he does seem to be able to externalize, to project or act out his internal contradictions in the themes and forms of his stories. Or rather, this is what happens when Kipling achieves his effects least overtly. As we have seen, however, he sometimes, indeed he too often short circuits the process and imposes on the narrative a political or social doctrine as to the way individuals and societies should relate to each other, instead of allowing resolutions to emerge from the creative act itself.

That this is something Conrad avoids is best illustrated by his use of symbol. Take, for instance, Stein's collection of lepidoptera in *Lord Jim*. All Conrad has him say of them is: "Look! The beauty—but that is nothing—look at the accuracy, the harmony. And so fragile! And so strong!"[2] To which the reader cannot help but add: "And formerly so wayward and free! And now so pinned down and categorized and imprisoned!" All these characteristics are doubly present, moreover, in the prize specimen captured as a direct result of Stein's being lured into, and escaping, an ambush. There is almost nothing these creatures could not symbolize, we feel; their relevance to the story seems both precise and open-ended. Forster's wasp, by contrast, is less a symbol than a peg from which to hang an idea. And Kipling's "Butterflies" makes explicit, through its allegory, what the preceding story, "Wire-less," merely implies. Indeed most of Kipling's symbols, whether a wound in the foot in "The Tender Achilles," the Wall in Parnesius's Roman stories, or the road, the wheel, and the mountains (to which the Lama must not lift up his eyes) in *Kim*, are half way to allegory, just as his allegories or parables or fables are often more than half way to propaganda.

On the surface, Conrad and Kipling are remarkably alike. Both write of the East and of Africa and use such locales as in some sense metaphors for the human condition, as well as making extensive use of other symbols. Both write, as no other modern author of comparable standing except perhaps Hemingway has done, about men of action. Both use the short story extensively. And both favor the device of a narrator. Yet in *The Heart of Darkness* Conrad uses Africa, in *Lord Jim* he uses a life of action and moments of paralysis (and butterflies), and in *Nostromo* he uses buried treasure, in each case as a compellingly suggestive image seeming to arise out of the characters' own efforts to arrive at a clearer understanding of the nature of their lives, rather than as a symbol whose meaning is imposed by the author. This in turn creates a sense of unity in Conrad's work—a sense that, like his characters, he is engaged in a constant search of this kind instead of, as is sometimes true in Kipling, presenting the reader with some hand-me-down vision of life. Similarly, so many of Conrad's novels began as short stories, and so many of his short stories might equally well have grown into novels, that any work of his seems to have the potential to become a major work, partly at least because it is integral to a larger unity. Finally, for Conrad to develop a constant though developing relationship between himself and a single recurring narrator not only makes for an interesting kind of stereoscopic vision, but implies a similar overall unity.

Forster's world is one of social and racial "aparthoods" which he attempts to connect, in the main through detached analysis. Kipling's is rife with opposing tendencies or dichotomies which he intuits in himself, in the first instance, and to which he seeks resolutions in the form of precarious states of equilibrium. There is still a real distinction between inner and outer in his work, however. The conflicting forces of the cosmos, of which we may be the microcosm, and to which in "Unprofessional" we may respond and attune ourselves, remain cosmic rather than becoming merely psychosomatic. The abyss has an external reality, however terrifyingly it may be mirrored in the mind. Conrad's view of the universe, though just as complex and fragmented, is by contrast profoundly monistic rather than polarized or Manichean. Man is himself the compendium of all he most fears. The

darkness, the undifferentiated chaos out of which he has clam-
bered and into which he may at any time relapse, he carries
within himself. "The mind of man is capable of anything—
because everything is in it, all the past as well as all the future."[3]
This is the unity which, ultimately, Conrad's work reflects.

To argue in this way that Conrad is a greater artist than
Kipling because of the greater consistency, almost the remorse-
lessness with which he explores, confronts, and compels us to
confront his vision of the human condition, might seem to
contradict what was said earlier about the unity to be found in the
apparent diversity of Kipling's *oeuvre*. And indeed, if mere
variety of subject matter and technique were all that detracted
from the coherence and integrity of Kipling's output, he might
well survive the comparison relatively unscathed. There is a unity
to Kipling's work when he is functioning wholly as an artist. But
he does not seem to trust his art sufficiently to say all that must be
said. And this results in a fatal inconsistency to his work which is
far more damaging than mere variety, arising as it does from a
readiness to use his art to serve those social and political beliefs
which are so often at odds with his deeper wisdom as an artist.
This is what leads to the crudely simplistic polemics of "A
Walking Delegate" and "The Mother Hive," to the complacent
exchange of inner-circle prejudices in "A Deal in Cotton" and
"The Honours of War," or to the enthusiastic and ingeniously
didactic absurdities of ".007" and "The Ship that Found Herself."
It is in the main because of this kind of unevenness in his work
that Kipling relegates himself to minor status when compared
with Conrad or James or Lawrence.

As Angus Wilson has argued, however, it is given to far fewer
writers to achieve the multiplicity and variety of Kipling's output
than to attain a more single-minded greatness.[4] To have reached,
as no English author since Dickens had done, a world-wide
readership of immense size and the widest possible intellectual
and social range, and to be quoted scores of times a day by people
who have no idea whom they are quoting, is to be honored in a
way many authors of the front rank might well envy. Moreover,
to have written at the same time one of the worlds's most

engaging novels of childhood, perhaps eight or ten of the hundred best short stories in the language, and a number of very fine poems, is arguably to redefine "major" and "minor" in a way that makes nonsense of all such classifications.

Notes and References

Chapter One

1. Charles Carrington, *Rudyard Kipling* (London, 1955), p. 506.

2. Rudyard Kipling, *Something of Myself* in *The Writings in Prose and Verse*, Outward Bound edition (New York, 1897–1937), 36:4. Subsequent page references in text.

3. T. S. Eliot, *A Choice of Kipling's Verse* (London, 1941), p. 23.

4. "Though many of his Indian tales present the bewildering complexity of the Indo-English relationship, Kipling never fully outgrew the innocence of his first six years; in a sense, the loyal and affectionate servant remained for him the prototype of the admirable Indian native." Louis L. Cornell, *Kipling in India* (New York, 1966), p. 3.

5. Lord Birkenhead, *Rudyard Kipling* (New York, 1978), pp. 25–26.

6. Ibid., p. 26.

7. Kipling, *Something of Myself*, p. 18.

8. Carrington, p. 20.

9. Angus Wilson, *The Strange Ride of Rudyard Kipling* (New York, 1978), p. 43.

10. Kipling, *Something of Myself*, pp. 63, 42.

11. Kipling admits that his verse satires, even when in agreement with the paper's editorials, were irreverent enough to speed his departure. *Something of Myself*, pp 71–73.

12. Kipling, *From Sea to Sea*, Outward Bound edition, 14:34.

13. Angus Wilson, pp. 170–71.

14. Roger Lancelyn Green, ed., *Kipling: The Critical Heritage* (New York, 1971), pp. 1, 16, 57, 69, 104, 127, 175.

15. Named "Naulakha," after Wolcott Balestier and Kipling's joint romance, *The Naulahka*; this time Kipling got the spelling right.

16. Angus Wilson, p. 174.

17. Kipling, "The English Flag," in *The Definitive Edition of Rudyard Kipling's Verse* (London, 1940), p. 221.

18. Birkenhead, p. 258.

19. Bruno Bettelheim, *The Informed Heart* (New York: Free Press of Glencoe, 1960), pp. 177–87.

Chapter Two

1. Kipling, *Plain Tales from the Hills,* in *Writings in Prose and Verse,* Outward Bound ed., I: 10, 40, 142. Volume and page numbers in text for all subsequent quotations from the fiction.

2. Bonamy Dobrée, *Rudyard Kipling: Realist and Fabulist* (London, 1967), p. 22.

3. Elliot L. Gilbert in *The Good Kipling* (Athens, Ohio, 1972), p. 144, equates Brahm's sleep with Findlayson's opium trance in the course of a reading of this story to which I am much indebted.

4. Kipling, "The Mutiny of the Mavericks," 3:369.

5. J. H. Fenwick, "Soldiers Three," in *Kipling's Mind and Art,* ed. Andrew Rutherford (Stanford, Calif., 1964), pp. 243–44.

6. Gilbert, pp. 60–70.

7. Angus Wilson, p. 72.

8. My reading of the story is strongly indebted to Elliot Gilbert's, pp. 21–41.

9. Noel Annan, "Kipling's Place in the History of Ideas," in Rutherford, pp. 110–11, and Dobrée, p. 63.

10. Edmund Wilson, "The Kipling that Nobody Read," in *The Wound and the Bow* (New York, 1959), pp. 123–24.

11. Mark Kinkead-Weekes, "Vision in Kipling's Novels," in Rutherford, pp. 216–34.

12. Ibid., pp. 230–31.

13. Ibid., pp. 233–34.

14. Edmund Wilson, p. 126.

Chapter Three

1. Roger Lancelyn Green in *Kipling and the Children* (London, 1965), p. 179, reports that the idea of a giant crab making the sea rise and fall is taken from a Malayan folk tale.

2. Kipling, *The Jungle Book* and *The Second Jungle Book,* as published by Macmillan in London and Century Books in New York, each contained a mix of Mowgli and other stories. In the Outward Bound edition Kipling authorized collecting all the Mowgli stories in *The Jungle Book,* and adding "In the Rukh" from *Many Inventions.*

3. Rutherford, pp. 100–102.

4. See the author's "Kipling's Jungle Eden," *Mosaic* 7, no. 2 (1974):151–64.

5. J. M. S. Tompkins, *The Art of Rudyard Kipling* (London, 1959), pp. 70–71.

6. Rutherford, pp. 211–13.

7. Birkenhead, p. 243.

8. John Gross, ed., *Rudyard Kipling, the Man, his Work and his World*, (London, 1972), p. 114.

9. Birkenhead, p. 244.

10. Kipling's actual model for the poem was the more mercurial Jameson, partner of Rhodes in South Africa. Birkenhead, p. 232.

11. Rutherford, pp. 211–14.

12. Kipling, *Something of Myself*, p. 201. He makes the same claim on behalf of both Puck books; the difference is that he nowhere claims, on behalf of the *Jungle Books* and *Kim*, that he "worked the material in three or four overlaid tints and textures."

Chapter Four

1. Carrington, p. 158.

2. Rutherford, p. 202.

3. Ibid., p. 205.

4. "Poseidon's Law," preceding the story, states that sailors never tell lies at sea, but make up for it when ashore.

5. C. A. Bodelsen, *Aspects of Kipling's Art* (New York, 1964), pp. 141–42.

6. Kipling, *Something of Myself*, pp. 199–200.

7. C. S. Lewis, "Kipling's World," in *Kipling and the Critics*, ed. Elliot L. Gilbert (New York, 1965), p. 100.

8. The accompanying poem, "The Vinyard" (about laborers paid the same wage for arriving at the eleventh hour as those who worked all day), was clearly written at least two years later, and indicates the nationality of the neutral.

9. Henry James, in *Kipling: The Critical Heritage*, p. 69.

10. Angus Wilson, pp. 267–68.

11. The story's epigraph clearly implies that madness may result from seeing beyond the veil customarily between us and the ultimate powers of the universe, and allows us to interpret the streaks the lighthouse keeper sees everywhere on the sea's surface as an image of just such a forbidden glimpse.

12. Alan Sandison, "The Artist and the Empire," in Rutherford, p. 164.

13. Kipling, "In the Interests of the Brethren," 31:85, 77.

14. Kipling in Preface to *In Black and White*, 4:v-vi.

15. *Definitive Edition*, p. 756.

16. Kipling, "Buddha at Kamakura," in *Definitive Edition*, p. 93.

17. Eliot, p. 15.

Chapter Five

1. Angus Wilson, p. 315.

2. "Then said my Daemon... 'Treat it as an illuminated manuscript.'" *Something of Myself*, p. 201.

3. Edmund Wilson, pp. 150-51.

4. *Acts* 27:16-18.

5. J. I. M. Stewart, *Rudyard Kipling* (New York, 1966), p. 202.

6. Angus Wilson, p. 337.

7. First and last lines of "Gertrude's Prayer," which Kipling has "Modernized from the Chaucer of Manalace" (33:36).

8. Harvesting of hops.

9. "Goo' Lord A'mighty! Where did she come by *that* word? cried Mrs. Fettley; for a Token is a wraith of the dead, or, worse still, of the living" (31:137).

10. Bodelsen, pp. 63-64.

Chapter Six

1. *Definitive Edition*, p. 98. All quotations from same source, title in text.

2. Cf. the music for "On the Road to Mandalay."

3. Eliot, p. 11.

4. Ibid., pp. 9, 18, 14.

Chapter Seven

1. Cornell, p. 23.

2. Joseph Conrad, *Lord Jim* (London: Dent, 1946), p. 208 (ch. 20).

3. Joseph Conrad, *Youth, Heart of Darkness, The End of the Tether* (London: Dent, 1946), p. 96.

4. Angus Wilson, p. 343.

Selected Bibliography

PRIMARY SOURCES

Cohen, Morton, ed. *Rudyard Kipling to Rider Haggard: The Record of a Friendship*. London: Hutchinson, 1965.

The Definitive Edition of Rudyard Kipling's Verse. London: Hodder and Stoughton, 1940.

The Writings in Prose and Verse of Rudyard Kipling. New York: Charles Scribner's Sons, 1897–1937. The titles, vol. nos., and dates of publication of the prose works referred to are given below, together with alternative titles and dates for the Trade Edition (i.e., Doubleday [& McClure/Page/Doran], or Macmillan, Appleton, and Century Books, whose titles Doubleday took over between 1901 and 1921), and the Uniform Edition of Macmillan, London, as well as the abbreviations used in the index.

		Outward Bound	Trade	Uniform
1	*Plain Tales from the Hills (PTH)*	1897	1899	1899
2, 3	*Soldiers Three and Military Tales (ST)*	1897		
	Soldiers Three: The Story of the Gadsbys: In Black and White (ST)		1899	1899
4	*In Black and White (BW)*	1897		
5	*The Phantom Rickshaw and Other Stories (PR)*	1897		
6	*Under the Deodars: The Story of the Gadsbys: Wee Willie Winkie (UD)*	1897		
	Under the Deodars:			

	The Phantom Rickshaw:			
	Wee Willie Winkie (UD)		1899	
	Wee Willie Winkie:			
	The Phantom Rickshaw:			
	Under the Deodars (UD)			1899
	Life's Handicap (LH)		1899	1899
	Many Inventions (MI)		1899	1899
7	The Jungle Book (JB)	1897	1899	1899
8	The Second Jungle Book			
	(SJB)	1897	1899	1899
9	The Light that Failed	1897	1899	1899
10	The Naulahka	1897	1899	1899
12	Captains Courageous	1898	1899	1899
13, 14	The Day's Work (DW)	1899	1898	1899
15, 16	From Sea to Sea	1899	1899	1900
18	Stalkey & Co. (SC)	1900	1899	1899
19	Kim	1902	1901	1901
20	Just So Stories (JSS)	1903	1902	1903
22	Traffics and Discoveries (TD)	1904	1904	1904
23	Puck of Pook's Hill (PPH)	1906	1906	1906
24	Actions and Reactions (AR)	1909	1909	1909
25	Rewards and Fairies (RF)	1910	1910	1910
26	A Diversity of Creatures			
	(D of C)	1917	1917	1917
31	Debits and Credits (D & C)	1926	1926	1926
33	Limits and Renewals (LR)	1932	1932	1932
36	Something of Myself	1937	1937	1937

BIBLIOGRAPHIES

Chandler, Lloyd H. *A Summary of the Work of Rudyard Kipling.* New York: The Grolier Club, 1930. Useful for magazine publications.
Livingston, Flora V. *Bibliography of the Works of Rudyard Kipling.* New York: Edgar H. Wells, 1927.
————. *Supplement to Bibliography of the Works of Rudyard Kipling.* Cambridge, Mass.: Harvard University Press, 1938.

Stewart, James McG. *Rudyard Kipling: A Bibliographical Catalogue.* Edited by A. W. Yeats. Toronto: Dalhousie University Press and University of Toronto Press, 1959. The most up-to-date and comprehensive guide to the complexities of Kipling editions.

SECONDARY SOURCES

Amis, Kinglsey. *Rudyard Kipling and his World.* London: Thames and Hudson, 1975. The pictures are good.

Beresford, G. C. *Schooldays with Kipling.* New York: Putnam, 1936. Somewhat acerbic account by a contemporary.

Birkenhead, Lord. *Rudyard Kipling.* New York: Random House, 1978. Lively biographical study with some new insights, but offering no radical reinterpretation.

Bodelsen, C. A. *Aspects of Kipling's Art.* New York: Barnes and Noble, 1964. Includes much to disagree with.

Brown, Hilton. *Rudyard Kipling.* New York: Harpers, 1945. Readable older study.

Carrington, Charles E. *Rudyard Kipling.* London: Macmillan, 1955. Still the standard biography.

Cornell, Louis L. *Kipling in India.* New York: St. Martin's Press, 1966. A good guide to the early years.

Dobrée, Bonamy. *Rudyard Kipling: Realist and Fabulist.* London: Oxford University Press, 1972. Analyzes Kipling's ideas.

Dunsterville, Lionel Charles. *Stalky's Reminiscences.* London: Jonathan Cape, 1928. Much mellower version than Beresford's of schooldays with Kipling.

Eliot, T. S. *A Choice of Kipling's Verse.* London: Faber, 1941. Prefaced by the best introduction to Kipling's poetry.

Escarpit, Robert. *Rudyard Kipling: Servitudes et Grandeurs Impériales.* Paris: Hachette, 1955. A different perspective.

Gilbert, Elliot L. *The Good Kipling.* Athens: Ohio University Press, 1972. Fine, selective insights on a limited range of stories.

———, ed. *Kipling and the Critics.* New York: New York University Press, 1965. Fine collection of classic essays by T. S. Eliot, C. S. Lewis, Orwell, Trilling, etc.

Green, Roger Lancelyn. *Kipling and the Children.* London: Elek Books 1965. Covers much more than the children's books; informative.

————, ed. *Kipling: The Critical Heritage*. New York: Barnes and
    Noble, 1971. Indispensable survey.
Gross, John, ed. *Rudyard Kipling: the Man, his Work and his World*.
    Weidenfeld & Nicolson, 1972. Attractive, brief aricles, illustrated.
Kipling Journal. Issued by the Kipling Society, London, since 1927. A
    mine of varied information.
Mason, Philip. *Kipling, The Glass, The Shadow and The Fire*. London:
    Jonathan Cape, 1975. Popular style; comprehensive.
Moore, Katharine. *Kipling and the White Man's Burden*. London:
    Faber, 1968. Excellent introduction, especially to *Kim*.
Rao, K. Bhaskara. *Rudyard Kipling's India*. Norman: University of
    Oklahoma Press, 1967. Good background material.
Rutherford, Angus, ed. *Kipling's Mind and Art*. Stanford: Stanford
    University Press, 1964. Excellent combination of older, classic
    essays and fresh material. Includes analyses of the intellectual and
    social background, and fine critical studies.
Shahane, Vasant A. *Rudyard Kipling, Activist and Artist*. Carbondale
    and Edwardsville: Southern Illinois University Press, 1973. Perhaps
    the best Indian study of Kipling.
Shanks, Edward. *Rudyard Kipling, A Study in Literature and Political
    Ideas*. New York: Doubleday, Doran, 1940. Good representative
    older study.
Stewart, J. I. M. *Rudyard Kipling*. New York: Dodd, Mead & Co., 1966.
    Always interesting, often penetrating.
Sutcliff, Rosemary. *Rudyard Kipling*. New York: Henry Z. Walck,
    1961. A children's writer on the children's books.
Tomkins, J. M. S. *The Art of Rudyard Kipling*. London: Methuen,
    1959. Still the best overall critical study.
Trilling, Lionel. *The Liberal Imagination*. New York: Viking, 1951.
    Contains a classic "liberal" essay on Kipling.
Wilson, Angus. *The Strange Ride of Rudyard Kipling*. New York:
    Viking, 1978. Criticism and biography well balanced and integrated.
    Uneven but indispensable.
Wilson, Edmund. *The Wound and the Bow*. New York: Oxford
    University Press, 1959. Contains controversial but crucial, turning-
    point essay.

Index

The title of each short story is followed by an abbreviation (see bibliography) of the title of the volume in which it appears, first in the Outward Bound edition, and second (if different) in the Doubleday/Macmillan editions.